IMPERIAL RUSSIA, 1801-1917

Nicholas II and Alexandra driving in the Imperial Park of
Peterhof, St. Petersburg, 1897. *(Library of Congress)*

CONTENTS

CHAPTER I

RUSSIA IN THE FIRST HALF OF THE NINE-TEENTH CENTURY

THE RUSSIAN EMPIRE IN THE MAKING

In October, 1721, upon the conclusion of the peace treaty of Nystadt which registered Russia's decisive victory over Sweden, the grateful and admiring members of the Russian Senate presented their Sovereign with the title of "Pater Patriæ, Imperator, Maximus." Thus the Russian Empire officially came into being. But at the time of Peter the Great's death (1725) much remained to be done to transform the imperial idea into a living reality. Peter laid the structural foundations; he left to his successors the task of completing the building.

Under Peter the Empire had not yet reached its "natural boundaries" even within the limits of the great east-European plain. Of the three fundamental problems of Russian foreign policy inherited from his predecessors, he was able to solve only one. The shores of the Baltic were reached, and their possession by Russia was made secure. Peter was not successful, however, in his attempt to establish Russia on the shores of the Black Sea. Moreover, the western territories, which for several centuries had been a bone of contention between Russia and Poland, were still outside the boundaries of the Empire. Only during the reign of Catherine II were these vital questions finally settled to Russia's satisfaction. So long as they had remained unsettled, Russia's imperial position was insecure.

A similar lack of political stability was revealed by Russia's internal development. Up to the end of the eighteenth century the dynasty had no firm foundation. An unfortunate law of imperial succession, promulgated by Peter in 1722, permitting the sovereign to choose his own successor even outside of the reigning house, had opened the way for all kinds of unexpected developments. One might say that in eighteenth-century Russia the problem of succession played the same all-important part as in Tudor England. From Peter's death up to the accession of Catherine (1762) almost every change of sovereign was accompanied by a palace revolution. A direct line of succession was not established until after Catherine's death, and it was only under Paul I that the claims of the dynasty to the Russian throne received a legal basis (Law of Succession to the Throne, 1797).

In the eighteenth century the Russian monarchy, strong as it was, had no adequate administrative machinery at its disposal. The competence of the highest state institutions was ill-defined; even their relation to the supreme power was not clearly formulated. The Senate, for example, which had been established by Peter to supervise the whole administration, would at one time sink into insignificance only to acquire at some later period an importance almost overshadowing that of the Sovereign. The executive departments of the central government were also badly organized. The "Collegia,"[1] borrowed by Peter from Sweden, had soon become obso-

[1] The "Collegia" were state departments in charge of the various branches of administration. Unlike modern ministries each of which is usually under the supervision of a single man, the "Collegia" were presided over by boards of about twelve members all equally responsible for the conduct of affairs in their respective departments.

lete and their virtual elimination by the end of the century left a vacuum that had to be filled. Even worse was the condition of local administration. In this field Peter had achieved very little and what he did accomplish was perhaps the least successful part of his work. Nor were his immediate successors able to remedy the situation. It was not until the reign of Catherine II that Russia received a rather elaborate system of local government which, with slight modifications, was destined to endure up to the reforms of Alexander II.

In the cultural life of Russia, chaos and confusion prevailed throughout a considerable part of the eighteenth century. The old civilization of Muscovite Russia, which had begun to lose its unity and strength in the course of the seventeenth century, had received its death blow at the hands of the reforming Tsar. But a certain period of time had to pass before it could be replaced by another equally complete system of beliefs and ideas. Through the proverbial "window," an opening which Peter had cut in the wall that separated Russia from west-European culture, various foreign influences—German, Swedish, Dutch, French and English—began to pour into the country in an ever-increasing stream. The first results of this impact could not be otherwise than bewildering. Among the small group of educated Russians many lost their mental balance. The result was either a slavish imitation of foreign patterns carried to extremes or else an extraordinary mixture of new ideas and old habits. With few exceptions there was neither stability nor originality in the intellectual and moral make-up of the men of the period. Quite obviously, all that had been so eagerly and so rapidly borrowed from abroad had to be digested and assimilated before a truly national civilization could be erected on new foundations. At first even the necessary means of expression were badly lacking. Until the second half of the eighteenth century Russia possessed no adequate publishing facilities, no press, not even a properly developed literary language. Not until Catherine's reign were tangible results obtained in all these directions and the ground prepared for creative achievements.

THE EMPIRE IN THE NINETEENTH CENTURY

In the beginning of the nineteenth century we find the period of preparation completed and the Empire an accomplished and firmly established fact. Even at that time it was by far the largest state in Europe. It had spread all over the east-European plain from the Baltic and the Arctic Ocean in the north to the Black Sea and the Caspian in the south; in Asia it possessed the whole of Siberia. Further expansion during the nineteenth century made the territory of the Empire equal to one-sixth of the surface of the globe. These new acquisitions were Finland, the central region of Poland (in addition to the border provinces annexed by Russia in the course of the three Partitions), Bessarabia, Transcaucasia, Transcaspian and Central Asiatic territories, and the Amur and Maritime provinces in the Far East. Impressive as those gains were, they were less significant than the acquisitions of the preceding period. Nor was it necessary for Russia, in this new phase of her imperial expansion, to make the same strenuous efforts and to endure the same sacrifices as before.

With the advent of the nineteenth century Russia for the first time in her history felt secure. Her old rival Poland was for the time being completely eliminated. Sweden had apparently resigned herself to the loss of her Baltic supremacy. Russia's relations with Turkey had undergone a profound change, Russia no longer being on the defensive, but, on the contrary, developing an aggressive near-Eastern policy of her own. As far as Russia's Asiatic frontier was concerned, the conquest of the Caucasus and of Central Asia was achieved in a series of colonial wars which were scarcely felt in the center of the Empire. Finally, in the Far East, Russia did not meet with any strong antagonists up to the beginning of the present century and thus was able to extend her territory in that region practically without fighting. From the beginning of the nineteenth century on, Russia's position among European nations was no longer questioned. She was generally recognized as one of the great European powers and she began to play an active, at times even a decisive, part in European affairs.

The territorial and ethnographic composition of the Empire was highly complex. Its nucleus was the old Tsardom of Moscow—the center, the north and the southeast of the European Russian plain, which had been gradually settled in the course of the preceding centuries by the Great Russian branch of the Russian people. Since the time of the Polish partitions the Russian sovereigns had also possessed all the lands that had been settled by the Little Russians (Ukrainians) in the Southwest and the White Russians in the West. Other acquisitions brought within the boundaries of the Empire territories with certain non-Russian groups: Finns, Baltic Germans, Latvians, Esthonians, Lithuanians, Poles, Moldavians, Georgians, Armenians, Tartars, and many other Asiatic tribes.

The Empire, however, was more homogeneous than many persons believe. Not only did the Great Russians represent the largest ethnographic group, but they formed a solid bloc in all the central regions of the Empire. And if we add to the Great Russians the Ukrainians and the White Russians, the numerical preponderance of the Russian stock over the non-Russian nationalities becomes even more decisive.[1] Both the Ukrainian and the White Russian national movements belong to a much later period. In the first half of the nineteenth century the problem of dealing with these groups was not particularly difficult. The same would be generally true of the more backward border provinces of the Empire where, as in the Caucasus, in the Transcaspian territories and in Central Asia, the imperial administration, with all its mistakes and deficiencies, was undoubtedly a civilizing force.

An infinitely more difficult problem was presented by the western provinces of the Empire. Here the imperial government had to deal with populations in many respects on a higher level of civilization than the Russians and with a tradition of independent or semi-independent existence behind them. Of these the Poles and the Finns were, of course, the outstanding examples. For some time both Poland and Finland retained a special status within the Empire. The Russian government recognized their privileges until the latter came into an acute conflict with the growing centralizing tendencies of the imperial administration; then they were either curtailed or abolished. Here the imperial régime was a failure. To the end of its existence it was not able to establish a permanent *modus vivendi* that would be satisfactory to both sides.

[1] On the eve of the World War there were in the Russian Empire about 80 million Great Russians, over 20 million Little Russians, and over 10 million White Russians, the three groups together counting over 120 millions out of the whole population of about 180 millions.

Another difficulty faced by the imperial administration was that of the enormous distances that separated one part of the Empire from another. This difficulty was felt very acutely throughout the first half of the nineteenth century when the ways of communication remained but feebly developed. The first paved highway between St. Petersburg and Moscow was completed in 1830 and thirty years later Russia still had only a little over five thousand miles of such roads. The first railroad was built in 1838 and during the next few decades railroad building progressed rather slowly: in 1867 all the railroad lines in Russia formed less than three and a half thousand miles. It is hardly necessary to point out that this state of affairs was a tremendous obstacle to the smooth and efficient functioning of the imperial machinery. When Alexander I died in Taganrog, in November, 1825, it took one week for the news of his death to reach St. Petersburg. One can easily imagine the situation when less important matters were involved. The more remote provinces of the Empire were, of course, particularly affected. Because of this lack of adequate means of communication Siberia, for instance, remained throughout the nineteenth century a thinly populated colony. It was not until the construction of the Trans-Siberian railroad, in the early years of the twentieth century, that this vast region became an integral part of the Empire.

LEGACY OF THE PAST: AUTOCRACY, NOBILITY, SERFDOM

The government of the Empire in the early nineteenth century was an absolute monarchy, not subject to any constitutional limitations and not limited in practice by any rival institutions or strongly entrenched social groups. Born simultaneously with the formation of a national

state in Russia, the autocracy [1] owed its continued existence and the gradual growth of its power to the exigencies of national defense and imperial expansion. Since
the days of Peter the Great it had lost its earlier semi-
religious and patriarchal character, but it did not abdicate any of its powers. If anything, it became even
stronger than it had been before. The old feudal aristocracy had passed away, the traditional council (Duma) of
the boyars had been abolished, the National Assembly
(*Zemski Sobor*) had disappeared, and the Church had
lost its independence; the autocracy alone remained.

In the course of the eighteenth century the Russian
autocracy became thoroughly westernized. It was now a
Grand Monarchy of the same type which had arisen in
western Europe during the first centuries of the modern
period. It stood in particularly close relationship to the
German monarchies of the Hapsburgs and the Hohenzol-
lerns. Its psychology was practically the same as that in
Berlin and in Vienna. Its ideal was a "regulated state"—
an essentially western conception—and it liked to attrib-
ute to itself a civilizing mission within the boundaries of
the Empire.

Nor was this an altogether empty claim. It was an
autocrat who in the early part of the eighteenth century
carried through a sweeping cultural reform and laid the
foundations on which modern Russian civilization gradually arose. And after Peter the Russian autocracy, irrespective of the personal qualities of its representatives,
continued on many occasions to take the lead in the cultural development of the country. Catherine II is, of
course, an outstanding example. Whatever one may
think of the defects of her policies, one must admit that

---

[1] Autocracy is used in this study to mean the traditionally unlimited powers of the crown vested in the person of the Tsar.

her patronage of arts and letters, her interest in education, her measures to promote social welfare, give her the right to be considered an "enlightened despot." Alexander I tried to exemplify enlightened despotism of this type when he ascended the throne in 1801.

The Russian Empire of the early nineteenth century inherited from the preceding period not only its form of government, but also its social organization. At the top of the social ladder stood the first estate in the country, the nobility. By this time there were very few noble families left which could trace their origin back to the old feudal aristocracy of medieval Russia. The new nobility was of a more recent origin. It gradually grew out of that class of "military service men" which the autocracy had created in the course of the sixteenth and seventeenth centuries for the purposes of national defense and imperial administration. During the reign of Peter the Great the nobles still were merely "royal servants," obliged to serve the government to the utmost of their capacity. In the course of the eighteenth century, however, they succeeded in gradually getting rid of this obligation while retaining, and even greatly increasing, their privileges. During the reign of Catherine II they became a privileged order, enjoying special economic and social rights which were no longer conditioned upon service and which were embodied in a charter granted to them by the sovereign (1785). The nobles were freed from both personal taxation and compulsory military service and they were also exempt from corporal punishment. They had the exclusive right of owning serfs and, up to 1801, they even enjoyed a monopoly of land-ownership. By the same charter of 1785 they received a corporate organization with the right to hold assemblies for the discussion and management of their affairs. They were also per-

mitted to elect their own officers (marshals of the nobility) in each province and district.

Important as these privileges were, they were not meant
to free the nobles from governmental control. Nor were
they based on a constitutional foundation. The charter
that had been given to the nobles by an autocratic sovereign could be taken away from them by another autocrat
(it actually was abolished by Paul I only to be restored
later by Alexander I). Thus the nobles' privileges by no
means constituted a limitation of autocracy: they were
social and economic, not political. If under Catherine II
the nobles played an all-important part in the government, this was due to the peculiar conditions of the time
—the necessity for a sovereign who had but a doubtful
legal claim to the throne to base her power on the support of the nobility. Neither Paul, nor Alexander I, nor
Nicholas I felt entirely dependent on this support and
no one of them can be truly called a "nobleman's tsar."

And yet, with all these reservations, it still must be admitted that, because of its social importance, the nobility
certainly exercised great influence in state affairs. Economically it was by far the strongest group in Russia so
long as landownership remained the chief source of wealth
in the country. The nobles alone constituted "society" in
the limited sense of the word, shining at the imperial
court and dominating the social life both in the urban centers and in the country districts. Well into the nineteenth century the nobility and the educated class remained almost synonymous terms. It was from their
ranks that most of the officers in the army and officials in
the civil administration were recruited. In the provinces
they were supreme up to the second half of the nineteenth
century. Not only did they possess patrimonial jurisdiction over the serf population of their estates, but as a

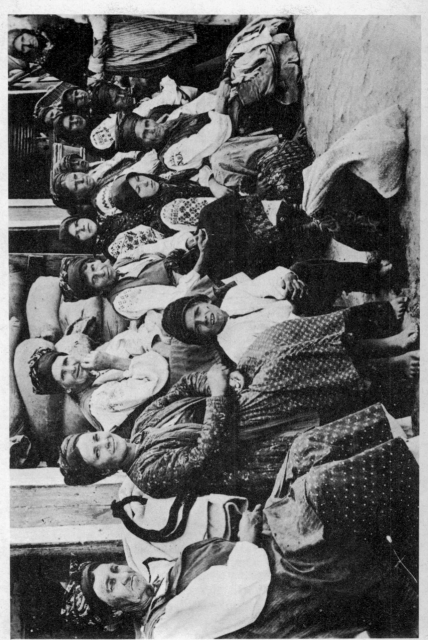

Russian peasants, nineteenth century. (*Library of Congress*)

Richelieu Street, Odessa, 1898. *(Library of Congress)*

rule they also held all the important offices of local administration.

The basis for the economic and social predominance of the nobility was serfdom, another institution that was a legacy of the past. Together with autocracy and the new nobility serfdom developed in that period of Russian history when a national state was being formed under the leadership of Moscow. Its appearance was due partly to economic causes which tended to increase the material dependence of the peasants upon the landlords. But this economic process was greatly strengthened and accelerated by a governmental policy which had both financial and military aims in view. The peasants were by far the largest group of taxpayers in the country and they alone were able to furnish the labor which was necessary for cultivating the lands of the "military service men." To insure the collection of taxes and the cultivation of lands the government wanted to check the migrating tendencies of the Russian peasants, to make them stay where they were, in other words to attach them to the soil. By the middle of the seventeenth century the process of enserfment had been completed. It remained for the eighteenth century to extend serfdom territorially and to make its bonds stronger.

By the beginning of the nineteenth century the authority of the landlords over their serfs became in fact all-embracing and almost unlimited. The landlord had the right to dispose of the person of his serfs: to sell them, to mortgage them, to give them away as a gift. He also had the right to exploit his serfs' labor without compensation. Some of them he would retain in his household as domestic servants, while the majority would be employed as laborers on his land. Or he might substitute for this *corvée* a monetary contribution—a kind of quit-rent—

paid to him by the serfs out of their earnings. Moreover, the landlord exercised police authority over his serfs and he was their sole judge in all but grave criminal cases. The government, however, did not abdicate entirely in the landlord's favor. His was the duty to provide food for his serfs in the periods of bad harvest and famine. A legal limit was set to the exploitation of serfs' labor: as far as the *corvée* was concerned, three days a week was officially proclaimed to be the maximum (1797), although in a great many cases the landlords disregarded the government's legislation. Finally, the landlords were prohibited by law from maltreating their serfs. But again, as in the case of excessive exploitation, the law was far from being always enforced and many offenders undoubtedly remained unpunished.

Between the nobility at the top and the peasantry at the bottom of the social ladder stood the middle classes of the Russian society—various categories of city inhabitants and the clergy. Neither in numbers [1] nor in influence were these groups particularly important. The relative weakness of the middle classes remained one of the outstanding features of Russian social organization up to the very end of the imperial régime; it was, of course, even more pronounced at the beginning of the nineteenth century. Urban life was still but feebly developed, and no strong and influential bourgeoisie of the west-European type existed. Under the law the higher categories of the merchants enjoyed some of the privi-

[1] At the end of the eighteenth century the peasants constituted 94.5 per cent of the population, the city inhabitants less than 3.5 per cent, the nobility a little over 1 per cent and the clergy 1 per cent. Of the whole peasantry, 55 per cent were serfs belonging to private landlords while the rest were crown serfs or free peasants.

leges that belonged to the nobility: like the nobles they were exempt from personal taxation, compulsory military service, and corporal punishment. Nevertheless, their social status remained an inferior one. As a class, they had no voice in matters of government. They did not play an important part in the cultural life of the country and they did not belong to "society." They remained a group apart, almost a caste, the young men rarely marrying outside of their own class and, as a rule, inheriting from their fathers both their social status and their occupation.

The same would be true of the clergy. Although they benefited from similar exemptions, it is impossible to see in them a privileged order. With the exception of a small number of the higher clergy, the social position of the group was a humble one, while the life of the parish priests in country districts did not differ to any noticeable degree from that of the peasants.

NEW TENDENCIES—POLITICAL IDEAS AND ECONOMIC DEVELOPMENT

Russian history is rich in contradictions. The one that was brought about by Russia's westernization is perhaps particularly striking. In opening the way to west-European influences the Russian autocracy was guided chiefly by considerations of a practical nature: it wanted first of all to strengthen national defense and to improve the machinery of government. But by pursuing this course it inevitably fostered the development of new tendencies which ultimately were bound to undermine its foundations. Thus, in a way, the autocracy was working for its own destruction.

To confine the process of westernization to the borrowing of west-European technique, while preserving intact

Russia's cultural isolation, was practically impossible. Western technique and western ways of living were inevitably followed by western ideas. And among these were ideas of constitutional government, civil equality and personal liberty. Under Catherine II the government itself sponsored for a while the spread in Russia of the French philosophy of "Enlightenment"; the writings of Montesquieu, Voltaire, Diderot and other Encyclopedists received the sovereign's stamp of approval. It is true that Catherine succeeded in combining an intense admiration for the principles of French philosophy with an equally strong conviction that autocracy was the only possible form of government in Russia. It is also true that her original enthusiasm for liberal ideas cooled down considerably after the outbreak of the French Revolution and, by the end of her life, almost completely disappeared. But not all of her subjects were ready to draw conclusions from the precepts of their French teachers similar to those drawn by the Empress, nor were they willing to stop when she wanted them to go no further. In the second half of the eighteenth century "Voltairianism" became quite an important feature in the intellectual life of the small group of educated Russians.

Another powerful influence was that of Free Masonry with its ideas of universal brotherhood and its emphasis upon civic duty. With many persons it was nothing but a pose or a passing intellectual fashion; but there was also a minority of sincere and serious-minded men for whom the new ideas had a vital and permanent significance. Already in Catherine's time we see the formation in Russia of a liberal public opinion and the beginnings of political opposition. It is not without justification that Novikov and his group of Moscow Masons, on the one hand, and Radishchev with his famous book, "A Journey from

St. Petersburg to Moscow" (1790), on the other, are considered as precursors of the Russian *intelligentsia* of a
later day.

All three bases of the traditional social and political order were made subject to attack and criticism.
To the principle of autocracy was opposed the ideal of
constitutional government. The predominance of the nobility was disputed in the name of civil equality; serfdom was attacked as an intolerable social injustice. So
far the opposition was confined merely to a small group
of educated men and it took the form of a literary crusade rather than that of organized political activity. But
even in this form it was significant as the beginning of
a movement which grew uninterruptedly, increasing in
strength and in volume until it resulted in an open conflict between the government and the liberal section of
public opinion. In the eyes of these men autocracy had
ceased to be an historical necessity. With imperial expansion completed in its main outlines and with security
from foreign attack more or less guaranteed, there seemed
to be no longer any justification for a permanent dictatorship. And with the development of national culture the
civilizing mission of autocracy began to be questioned as
well. The educated Russians became of age and began
to resent governmental tutelage. Before long they would
demand for themselves a share in the management of
national affairs.

While intellectual progress was leading men to challenge the wisdom and validity of the existing social and
political order, important changes were gradually taking
place in the economic life of the country. Ultimately
these changes were bound to undermine serfdom and with
it the social predominance of the landowning nobility.

Many decades still separated Russia from the period when she was to feel the full strength of the Industrial Revolution with its inevitable and far-reaching consequences. But even in the beginning of the nineteenth century one can clearly discern some new phenomena which were preparing the ground for this Revolution. Accumulation of capital inside of the country and the increasing participation of Russia in international trade led to a more rapid growth of industry and commerce. Under the influence of this development agriculture, although still based on serfdom, began to change its character. The landlords were becoming more and more interested in producing for the market. This was particularly true in the fertile South where agricultural production, thanks to Russia's rapidly increasing exports of grain, was greatly stimulated. In the North, where the land was not so fertile, the landlords displayed a constantly growing desire to turn from agriculture to other fields of economic activity. Here they would employ the labor of their serfs in the factories built on their estates, or else derive their income chiefly, if not exclusively, from their serfs' earnings.

Both in the South and in the North the economic system based on serfdom was trying not without some success to adapt itself to new conditions. But as time went on, it became more and more obvious that in the long run serfdom was incompatible both with industrial progress and the growth of capitalistic agriculture. The productivity of serf labor was low and it could not be substantially raised. Scarcity of free labor was a serious obstacle to the further development of industry. A conflict between serfdom and the vital needs of the nascent Russian capitalism was becoming inevitable.

GOVERNMENTAL POLICIES UNDER ALEXANDER I (1801-1825) AND NICHOLAS I (1825-1855)

Such were the general conditions which Alexander I and Nicholas I both had to face. It must be admitted that theirs was an extremely difficult task. On the one hand, they inherited firmly established political traditions—traditions which they considered it their duty to preserve. On the other hand, they were confronted with the development of new tendencies which were a natural result of Russia's changed international position. These new tendencies were inevitably coming into a conflict with the old order of things. Both of these rulers tried, each in his own way, to meet the demands of new times without sacrificing the foundations of the old political system. In some respects this attempt was a partial success, in others a complete failure. If there were at times glaring contradictions in the governmental policies under Alexander and Nicholas, this was perhaps unavoidable: the contradictions lay in the situation itself.

The chief concern of the Russian government of that period was first to put its own house in order, that is, to establish the properly organized and efficient administrative machinery which had been previously lacking. As a result, administrative reform took precedence over all other problems of governmental policy. The aim was to make the Russian government a "well-regulated monarchy" which henceforward would rest on the firm foundation of law, to create a system of governmental agencies with clearly established spheres of activity, and to define their relation to the supreme power in a way that would make any further uncertainty impossible. This aim was at least partially achieved. It was in the first quarter of the nineteenth century that modern Russian bureaucracy

was born. It was also during this period that modern
notions of law first found their way into Russia, and that
the principle of separation of powers was more or less
consistently applied. Initiative in legislation belonged
to the sovereign alone, but each law had to be first discussed in the Council of State (1810), a body of governmental experts appointed by the Emperor, which took the
place of the Senate as the highest state institution. The
executive branch of the government was represented by
the Ministries which were finally organized in 1811.
These were state departments of the usual west-European
type, each with a well-defined competence and each under
the direction of a minister who was personally responsible
for the legality of its actions. Somewhat later the reform of central government found its necessary comple-
tion in the publication of a systematic code of Russian
laws (1832). Both the codification of laws and the organization of the Russian bureaucracy on a modern basis
were principally the work of one man, Michael Speranski
(1772-1839), whose administrative genius remains perhaps unequaled in Russian history.

Even after this work had been completed, there still
existed a wide gap between the ideal and reality. Side
by side with regular legislative procedure there developed
a practice of exceptional legislation, and the administration did not always feel itself bound to keep within the
limits of law. It must also be remembered that both the
reform of local government and that of the judiciary had
to wait until the second half of the nineteenth century.
And yet, in spite of these limitations, the system of central government as organized in that period was an im-
mense improvement upon the more or less chaotic conditions that had prevailed in the eighteenth century.
With slight modifications it persisted almost intact up

to the constitutional reform of 1905-1906 and, from the purely technical point of view, it proved to be fairly efficient.   Moreover, to use the words of a modern historian, there was from that time "a right and a wrong way of conducting government business in Russia"; this in itself was not a mean achievement.

While these changes in the central administration were taking place, autocracy lived on intact. In the days of Alexander, however, the possibility of its transformation into limited monarchy had been repeatedly discussed in governmental circles. In fact, this discussion had been encouraged by the sovereign himself. Brought up in a "republican spirit" and professing his admiration for liberal principles, Alexander again and again returned to the idea of a written constitution for Russia only to drop it each time it approached realization. For example, he discussed a constitutional charter to be granted to the Russian people with those intimate friends of his who formed his "Unofficial Committee" in the first years of his reign. It was at his express command that several years later (1809) Speranski prepared an elaborate draft of a constitution which remained one of the most famous documents in the history of Russian political thought. And again, in 1819-1821, another of his collaborators, Novosiltsev, prepared at the Emperor's request a project for an imperial constitution, this time on a federalist basis. It is well known that none of these attempts led to any practical results and in each case this was due to hesitation on the part of Alexander himself. To accuse Alexander of mere hypocrisy would be unjust. To explain the failure of his constitutional projects on the basis of a supposed radical change in his views—a change that in the middle of his life transformed him from a liberal into a reactionary—would be to simplify the problem. The fact was that throughout his life liberalism and respect for autocracy continued to co-exist in his complex and self-contradictory nature. His liberalism did not include any notion of real self-government, and, while he wanted a constitution, he desired one that would not limit the sovereign's freedom of action.

There were none of these contradictions in Nicholas' attitude towards the problem. With him a deeply rooted belief in the sanctity of his office and a whole-hearted devotion to the principle of autocracy were combined with a feeling that it was his duty to combat the "spirit of revolution" both at home and abroad. Domestic and foreign events alike tended to confirm him in this attitude. In Russia his accession was greeted by an abortive attempt at a revolution (the Decembrist rising of 1825), and in western Europe he was destined to witness the outbreaks of 1830 and 1848. The guiding motive of his policy became, therefore, a vigorous defense of "legitimacy" in Russia as well as outside of her borders. Yet in spite of this Nicholas, no less than Alexander, was painfully conscious of the outstanding evils of Russian life and he was sincerely anxious to see the situation improved. His illusion was that it would be possible to achieve this aim while leaving intact the foundations of the existing order. In other words, he wanted reforms, not Reform. And even these he was determined to carry through by bureaucratic means alone, without any coöperation on the part of those independent public elements which he so deeply distrusted. Hence the numerous "secret committees" which throughout the first part of his reign were almost incessantly discussing various reforms. Hence also the prodigious growth under Nicholas of what might be called the emperor's "personal government." With the exception of Peter the Great, no other Russian sovereign ever went personally into so many details of administration and reserved for himself such a large share of governmental business.   This is why in Nicholas' time "His Majesty's Own Chancery" became one of the most important state institutions.   Another outgrowth of the same tendency was the practice, greatly favored by Nicholas, of occasionally sending out some trusted generals, usually his personal aides-de-camp, on inspection tours into the provinces.   The task of these modern *missi dominici* was to correct the mistakes and abuses of local administration, which obviously could not be effectively controlled through regular channels.   In a way this procedure was a striking testimony to the inherent weakness of the imperial system.

The problems of general policy were greatly complicated by the paradoxical situation in some of the border regions of the Empire.   The Polish problem was, of course, the thorniest.   In 1815 the Kingdom of Poland became a part of the Russian Empire while retaining in its internal life an autonomous status.   Poland was granted a constitution which in its day was perhaps the most liberal in Europe.   She had her own legislative assembly, her own administration and a charter of civil liberties.   Here was a field where Alexander could try out his constitutional theories—and the experiment was not a success.   Because of Alexander's inability to play consistently the part of a constitutional monarch, and also because of the unwillingness on the part of the Poles to give up the idea of a restored and independent Poland, the relations between the Russian sovereign and his Polish subjects became very strained by the end of Alexander's life.   Moreover, it seemed also to many in Russia that the Empire could not continue to be partly autocratic and partly constitutional.   Alexander himself was undoubtedly aware of the contradiction when he instructed Novosiltsev to draw up a constitutional project which contemplated reorganization of the empire on a federalist basis. As nothing came out of the attempt, the realization of the other alternative became more likely: if one could not make Russia constitutional, one could deprive Poland of her constitution. This task fell upon Nicholas. When, in 1830, the Poles rose in a general rebellion to win back their lost provinces and their independence, Nicholas felt himself free to break the compact. After the insurrection had been suppressed the constitution was abolished. On paper the Poles still retained a certain degree of autonomy, but actually for the rest of Nicholas' reign Poland was placed under a military régime. The Finns and the Baltic Germans managed to preserve their privileged status more or less intact up to a much later period, while Transcaucasia and Bessarabia were governed almost from the outset as mere Russian provinces.

Next to the reform of the imperial administration the problem of serfdom occupied the most important place in the governmental policies of the first half of the nineteenth century. It certainly was no less complicated nor less pregnant with contradictions. Both Alexander and Nicholas realized that the situation was becoming less and less satisfactory and that something had to be done to improve it. The new economic factors, which have been already indicated, worked incessantly and with increasing strength to undermine the foundations of serfdom, while the moral protest against human bondage was also growing among the advanced groups of educated Russians. The serfs themselves were restless, and there were no less than 556 serious outbreaks during the thirty years of Nicholas' reign. From the beginning of the century the government was contemplating an eventual liberation of serfs, but again and again it became appalled by the magnitude of the task, dreading grave and perhaps fatal disturbances in the social and economic life of the country. Opinion prevailed that liberation of the serfs had to be accompanied by a land settlement, and this was impossible without at least a partial alienation of the landlords' property. Before this prospect of an attack upon the vested interests of the landed gentry even the all-powerful Russian autocracy would naturally shrink. This is why the government preferred a scheme of gradual emancipation with the initiative coming from the landlords themselves. A law published by Alexander in 1803 permitted the landlords, if they so desired, to liberate their serfs and to provide them with land in return for monetary compensation. The results of the law were negligible because the majority of the landlords had no desire to part with their property and the peasants, as a rule, had no money to pay for the land. In 1842 the government of Nicholas tried to make the procedure easier for both sides: under the terms of this new law the landlords could grant the peasants permanent use of the land while themselves retaining the title to the property, and the peasants could pay for the land by specified services to the landlord. But this law also, like its predecessor, was largely inoperative.

Under the circumstances all that remained possible for the government to do was to introduce specific and partial improvements. Laws were passed, for instance, that prohibited either the sale of serfs at public auctions or the separation of members of the same family, and efforts were made to check the arbitrary rule of the landlords by defining the punishments which they could legally inflict upon their serfs. Under Nicholas the position of the numerous crown serfs was somewhat improved as a result of certain administrative changes. More important measures were taken in connection with the peasantry of those border regions where the landlords were of a non-Russian origin. In the Baltic provinces the serfs were made personally free without, however, obtaining any land. In the western provinces the duties of the serfs towards their landlords were defined by law, a substantial improvement.

As to the general problem of serfdom, the government continued to move in a kind of vicious circle, always conscious of the necessity of reform and yet unwilling to attempt a radical solution. Nobody summed up the situation better than Nicholas himself. "There is no doubt," he said in 1842, "that serfdom in its present state is an evil which is felt by all and is obvious to all, but to touch it now would be, of course, even a more disastrous evil."

When we turn now to the educational policy of the government, we find an equally paradoxical situation. That the widest possible spread of education in Russia was a vital necessity was not doubted by the responsible men in the government. But strong misgiving was often felt as to the ultimate results of the educational process. It seemed to the governing circles that special precautions had to be taken lest new ideas undermine the loyalty of the people toward established authority; in pursuing this course, obviously, they were gravely compromising the success of their own educational endeavors. In the early days of Alexander's reign a very promising start was made in the field of public instruction. Under the guidance of the newly established Ministry of Education, the first institution of its kind in Russian history, substantial progress was achieved in connection with both the higher and secondary schools. Instead of the one university with which Russia had been satisfied until the end of the eighteenth century, there were now six. To these were added in the course of Nicholas' reign some technical schools such as the Institutes of Technology in St. Petersburg and Moscow. During the first half of the nineteenth century the number of secondary schools was also growing considerably, but the development of primary education still lagged far behind. In the beginning of the century a fair amount of freedom was allowed in teaching and no attempt was made to apply class discrimination to the educational system. The situation changed for the worse in the later part of Alexander's reign and a reaction set in which affected the universities in particular. This was part of a general system of censorship which aimed at controlling the spiritual life of the nation and at combating all dangerous deviations from the officially approved dogma. From that time on and until the period of reforms was inaugurated by Alexander II, this system of strict governmental supervision both of education and of literature remained an outstanding feature of Russian life. It became particularly strong under Nicholas I who, as we know, considered it his sacred duty to combat the "revolutionary spirit." It was under Nicholas that measures were taken to exclude the lower classes from the higher grades of the educational system. There was an obvious contradiction between the desire of the government to promote education and its attempt to suppress freedom of thought. What it wanted was, in the words of a contemporary, "a fire that would not burn."

CIVILIZATION AND PUBLIC OPINION

Meanwhile a great change was taking place in the cultural life of the country. The period of apprenticeship was over; the first quarter of the nineteenth century saw the birth in Russia of a new national civilization. With few exceptions the men of the eighteenth century had been either mere pupils of western Europe or, at their best, somewhat timid beginners in the ways of independent cultural endeavor. The educated Russians of the early nineteenth century were their teachers' equals in many, if not in all respects. They were sure of themselves and of their right to say what they wanted in their own national idiom. They still employed western forms of expression, but they used them with freedom and in a spirit of critical discrimination. And on all that they borrowed from western Europe they began to leave an unmistakable mark of their own nationality.

The first standard-bearers of modern Russian civilization belonged almost exclusively to the privileged minority. It was not until the thirties of the nineteenth century that the representatives of the non-privileged classes made themselves heard in various fields of intellectual and artistic activity. But even as late as the middle of the century the cultural life of Russia still was dominated by the nobility. This is why one usually speaks of the civilization of the period as that of the landowning gentry. It flourished in particular around the court of St. Petersburg, in the literary salons of Moscow and in the "noblemen's nests" of the country districts. Its existence was based upon a social injustice, but the realization of this fact should not make us blind to its peculiar charm and beauty. For the visible expression of this beauty one can turn to the architecture of the period. West-European in its origin, it was a creative adaptation of the neo-classical "Empire" style of the late eighteenth and early nineteenth centuries. More formal and majestic in the official buildings of St. Petersburg, it acquired a much more intimate and decidedly Russian character in Moscow and on the provincial estates of the gentry where it seemed to harmonize to perfection with the landscape of the Russian countryside.

But the most striking triumphs of the new Russian civilization were achieved in the field of literature. Taken as a whole, the reigns of Alexander and Nicholas remain the Golden Age in Russian literary history. The period saw both the full bloom of Russian poetry and the rise of the Russian novel. Pushkin, Russia's greatest poet, began to write under Alexander, but reached the summit of his literary career under Nicholas. Lermontov, another great poet, belongs entirely to Nicholas' time, and so does Gogol, the father of the Russian novel. And the last years of Nicholas' reign were marked by the publication of the first works of Turgenev, Tolstoi, Dostoevski, and Goncharov. It was also during the same reign that the national school of Russian music was born with Glinka, and that Alexander Ivanov completed his "Christ Appearing Before the People," perhaps the first work of genius in the history of modern Russian painting.

That arts and letters flourished in spite of a system of strict governmental censorship is not perhaps surprising. Literary and artistic activity does not seem to stand in any direct relation to the form of government or to general political conditions. Democratic Athens and absolutist France alike gave birth to great and enduring civilizations. What is surprising is the fact that in the autocratic Russia of that time prohibitive measures, far-reaching and drastic enough, proved to be unable to check the progress of a liberal public opinion. A number of circumstances combined to permit liberalism to make a fair start in the early part of Alexander's reign. The liberal pronouncements of the sovereign himself and rumors as to the contemplated constitutional reform played the part of a powerful stimulus in this direction. Then came the Napoleonic wars which brought a large number of educated Russians into direct contact with various currents of western political thought. Many Russian officers returned to their country after 1815 with an intense desire to see political changes introduced at home. The disappointment that followed the failure of all constitutional projects resulted in the formation of a loosely organized political opposition. The spectacle of the government sponsoring a constitutional régime in Poland and Finland, while reserving autocracy for the Russians themselves, added no little bitterness to this dissatisfaction. Such, in brief, was the genesis of the so-called movement of the Decembrists, the first attempt at a political revolution in modern Russian history (1825). The movement was doomed to fail because it was confined to a small group of educated men, because it was divided within itself between a moderate and a radical tendency, and, finally, because it was badly organized and did not possess a developed revolutionary technique. Yet even in its failure it made a very strong impression on public opinion and the Decembrists were regarded by later generations of Russian liberals and revolutionaries as the pioneers of freedom.

During the thirty years of Nicholas' reign autocracy remained supreme and nobody dared to come out in the open to challenge its formidable power. But if there was no political action, there was plenty of thinking, which became increasingly intense as a result of the impossibility of applying theories to life. Alexander Herzen, himself a contemporary, has called this period "an amazing time of outward slavery and inner liberation." At first, however, the thoughts of the generation that followed the Decembrists were not directed towards poli-

tics. They passed through a period of enthusiastic interest in abstract philosophical principles as expounded
by the German idealistic philosophy of the time. From
Schelling through Fichte to Hegel—such was the way
that was followed by the outstanding representatives of
"Young Russia" until the majority of them became for a
while "desperate Hegelians." But there was something
in the very intensity of their philosophical studies which
indicated from the outset that all these theories meant for
them much more than mere intellectual speculation. It
was in the debating "circles" of the period, centered
chiefly around the University of Moscow, that there were
formed some of the most characteristic features of the
later Russian *intelligentsia:* its idealism and also its im-
practicability, its emphasis upon theory and its unwillingness to compromise, its interest in ethical problems
and its desire to serve humanity. It was also in the
course of these discussions that young noblemen of progressive tendencies first joined hands with those representatives of the lower classes who began to find their
way into educated society. In the days to come these
new elements were destined to give the *intelligentsia* a
group-consciousness of its own and to contribute to the
triumph in its ranks of more radical tendencies. Of the
earlier members of this group Belinski, the first Russian
literary critic of note, was by far the most remarkable.
By turning literary criticism into a vehicle for carefully
veiled political and social propaganda he was able to exercise a powerful influence upon the youth of his generation,
thus defeating to a considerable extent the vigorous efforts of the censor.

In the forties of the nineteenth century we see the formation in Russia of strong currents of thought, already
somewhat political in nature. It was in those years that

the battle was raging between the Westerners and the Slavophils. The main theme of discussion was the meaning of Russian history and the future course of Russia's destiny. For the Westerners the difference between Russia and western Europe was one of degree only. Because of the unfavorable circumstances of her historical development Russia was behind the western nations in her political and social institutions as well as in her civilization. Fundamentally, however, she was passing through the same phases of historical evolution, and her task was to advance with redoubled energy along the road of westernization and to catch up with the more advanced nations of the western world. Westernism became, therefore, a cardinal tenet with all the groups of educated Russians who desired for their country a constitutional government. In their philosophy the Westerners, as a rule, were Rationalists, and their attitude towards religion was either hostile or indifferent. For the Slavophils, on the other hand, the difference between Russia and the western world was one of kind, not of degree. Russian history had been radically different from that of western Europe, and her civilization was based on entirely different principles. It was the difference between the Romano-Germanic world, on the one hand, and the Slavonic world, on the other (hence the name of the Slavophils). For the Slavophils Russia's original civilization, in which her Greek-Orthodox religion played an all-important part, was a cherished possession that should be by all means preserved intact. Instead of following the lead of western nations, threatened with inevitable decay, Russia was to say a new word in human history. More particularly, the evils of western industrialism could and should be avoided. In her peasant commune Russia had a highly valuable institution on the basis of which a better economic system, and one that would satisfy the demands of social justice, could be eventually erected. Neither was there a place in Russia for the west-European parliamentary constitutionalism. The peculiar Russian type of government was a benevolent autocracy assisted by an advisory popular body such as the National Assembly (*Zemski Sobor*) of the seventeenth century.

At first glance the Slavophil doctrine looked like a replica of the officially sponsored formula which read "Orthodoxy, Autocracy, Nationalism." This is why the Slavophils have been so often accused of reactionary tendencies. However, this is a serious mistake. The Slavophil doctrine, as expressed by its early exponents, was permeated with a broadly liberal spirit. The autocracy they were thinking about was not like that of Nicholas I, with its suppression of public opinion and glorification of bureaucratic control. It was a patriarchal and in a way even a democratic monarchy, serving the cause of social justice and based upon freely-given popular support. Similarly, the Slavophil's conception of Orthodoxy was that of a free and independent Church which would occupy a leading place in the country's spiritual life because of its inherent strength and not because of governmental protection. And finally, what they wanted was a spontaneous and untrammeled development of Russian nationality and not a rigid formula of official nationalism forced upon the country from above.

Here then was a common ground on which the Westerners and the Slavophils could meet. Both schools were in favor of public control over the bureaucracy, both were asking for personal liberty, and, above all, both insisted on the abolition of serfdom.

Another important phenomenon in the history of Russian political ideas of the period was the birth of Russian socialism. Its origin was also west-European, but in this case the predominant influence was French, not German. The writings of Saint-Simon and Fourier served as the starting point for the development of the Russian socialist doctrine. As yet this doctrine was of a purely theoretical nature and it was confined to a few intellectuals; nevertheless, it was in this very circle of literary men that theories were worked out which a few decades later became a source of inspiration for revolutionary activity. In their general outlook these early Russian socialists, of whom Alexander Herzen was the most outstanding representative, occupied a peculiar position midway between the Westerners and the Slavophils. They shared with the Westerners a critical attitude towards Russia's past and present as well as a preference for rationalistic philosophy, but they stood closer to the Slavophils in their distrust of west-European parliamentary democracy, in their belief that it was Russia's mission to bring a new message to the world, and also in their idealization of the peasant commune, which seemed to them the nucleus of a better social order. It is hardly necessary to add that the socialists were even more strongly opposed to the existing political régime than either the Westerners or the Slavophils.

THE CRIMEAN WAR AND THE COLLAPSE OF THE OLD ORDER

The reign of Nicholas ended in Russia's military and diplomatic defeat in the Crimean War (1853-1855), a war in which she had to face single-handed a strong coalition of west-European powers. The immediate origin of the war lay in the conflict between Russia's interests in the Near East with those of France and England. Russia wanted to establish her control over the Straits, and she claimed a right of protectorate over the Greek-Orthodox subjects of the Sultan, while neither the French nor the British were prepared to permit her ascendancy in the Near East. A contributing cause of no small importance was that feeling of distrust which had been aroused in the public opinion of western Europe by Russia's foreign policy in the first half of the nineteenth century.[1] This had been a policy of active intervention in west-European affairs, in the name of the Holy Alliance under Alexander and in defense of "legitimacy" under Nicholas. In both cases it inevitably clashed with the growing tendencies towards democracy and national independence which became so strongly pronounced in this period of European history. In 1830-31 Nicholas was vigorously opposed both to the July revolution in France and to the cause of Belgian independence; his suppression of the Polish rebellion made him extremely unpopular with the French and the British liberals whose sympathies were entirely on the Polish side. In 1848-49 he again attempted to combat the revolution in France, he came out against the constitutional movement both in Prussia and in Austria, he supported the Austrian government diplomatically and financially in its struggle with the Italian nationalists and he sent an army into the Austrian Empire to help Francis Joseph crush the Hungarian insurrection.[2] The result was that when the war broke out over the

[1] Russian interference in west-European international politics had been persistent since the days of Catherine the Great. Europe had not forgotten the presence of Russian troops on Napoleonic battlefields nor the presence of Russian influence at Vienna in 1815.

[2] These events strengthened the great fear of the Russian army which was widespread in Europe during the first half of the nineteenth century and constituted an important factor in the European appraisal of Russia and its purposes during that period. The Crimean War, needless to say, exploded the myth of the great strength of the Russian army.

Near Eastern question, it assumed in the eyes of west-European liberals the character of a crusade against autocracy and "oriental barbarism" in defense of freedom and civilization. To make Russia's isolation even more complete her own allies, Austria and Prussia, not only did not come to her assistance but assumed towards her an attitude that was far from being friendly. Fought under these circumstances, the Crimean War turned out to be extremely unfortunate for Russia. In spite of the bravery of her soldiers, Russia was defeated on her own territory chiefly because her army was poorly supplied and badly managed, while inefficiency prevailed in the rear. The outcome of the war was a sad blow to Russia's military and political prestige.

It was a sad blow also to the authority of the Russian government at home. How could it demand unquestioning obedience from its own subjects when it revealed itself impotent to protect Russia's place in international relations? And did not the war expose with painful obviousness all the crying evils of Russian life, the country's economic backwardness, the incompetence of bureaucracy, the dishonesty of many officials, and the general weakness of public spirit? The sense of national humiliation added new fuel to the fire of discontent which had been burning for years in the souls of many educated Russians. Among them opposition to the existing order of things became almost universal. The feeling that the old system was fundamentally wrong and that immediate reforms were a vital necessity was no longer confined to the liberal Westerners and Slavophils, but was also shared by many conservatives. Nicholas himself was forced to come to the conclusion that his régime was a failure. He died a bitterly disappointed monarch, leaving his son and successor a sadly deranged estate.

CHAPTER II

REFORM AND REACTION

(1855-1905)

THE REFORMS OF ALEXANDER II

THE reign of Alexander II (1855-1881) is a landmark
in Russian history; during this period there occurred a
series of far-reaching reforms which profoundly changed
the life of the country. Alexander II was not a reformer
by nature. But he was intelligent enough to be able to
read the signs of the times, and courageous enough, at
least during the early part of his reign, to subordinate his
personal feelings to considerations of state. Some of his
reforms suffered at the outset from compromise with
vested interests; others were distorted as a result of the
reaction which set in during Alexander's own life-time.
Because of these facts the "Great Reforms" have sometimes been harshly criticized and their wisdom has been
questioned in the light of subsequent developments. The
proper historical approach, however, is to judge them
on the basis of a comparison with the old order of things
which they were designed to modify. They stand this
test, and the customary division of nineteenth-century
Russian history into pre-reform and post-reform periods
seems to be fully justified.

By far the most important event of the reign of Alexander II was the abolition of serfdom (1861). Such an
act could hardly be postponed any longer. Economic
development and pressure of public opinion were steadily

undermining the foundations of serfdom while the rest-
lessness of the serfs made the government fear another
general peasant uprising. Like his predecessors, Alexander II began by trying to persuade the landlords to take
the initiative; accordingly he pointed out to them that it
was "better to abolish serfdom from above than to wait
till it begins to abolish itself from below." When, however, he saw that this initiative was slow in manifesting
itself and that the majority of the Russian nobles were
still clinging to the rights which they enjoyed under serfdom, he decided to take matters into his own hands. It
was the government which forced upon the unwilling nobility an open discussion of the reform, and it was the
government which declared in the early stages of this discussion that the emancipation must be accompanied by a
land settlement for the liberated serfs. The reform was
actually carried through by the autocratic sovereign, in
coöperation with a few enlightened bureaucrats and the
liberal section of public opinion, against strong opposition on the part of the majority of the nobles. For three
years a fierce struggle went on over the terms of the pro-
posed settlement; if the final results were not entirely
satisfactory to the peasants they still were immeasurably
more advantageous to their interests than if the whole
matter had been left in the hands of the landlords.

The legal aspect of the reform, the abolition of human
bondage, stands out as its most conspicuous and, at the
same time, its most beneficial feature. The very fact that
over 40 millions of human beings were liberated goes
far to justify the description of the Emancipation as
"perhaps the greatest single legislative act in the world's
history." However, the economic side of the reform is
obviously open to criticism. Generally speaking, the
peasants retained in their hands that part of the land

which they had been permitted as serfs to use for their own maintenance. The landlords were compensated for the loss of this property by the state, but the peasants had to repay the sum to the Treasury in annual installments spread over a period of forty-nine years. Conditions varied with different localities and different groups of the peasantry, but in most cases the land allotments were too small, and the redemption payments proved to be too heavy a burden for the peasants. Even so the reform involved a forcible alienation of a very substantial part of the landlords' property, and in Russia the terms of the land settlement consequent upon the Emancipation were considerably more generous than they had been in west-European countries. One feature of this settlement, however, was rather unfortunate. As a rule the land was not given outright to individual peasants but was transferred to the village communes whose members were to receive equal allotments along with the right of periodical redistribution. In pursuing this course the sponsors of the reform were guided partly by interests of fiscal policy (the commune was made responsible for the payment of its individual members' taxes and redemption installments), and partly by a desire to prevent loss of land by the peasants and the formation of a rural proletariat. Subsequent developments showed, however, that the commune was not able to perform successfully the functions expected of it, while at the same time it became an obstacle to agricultural progress.

The Emancipation was highly significant not only in itself but also as a starting point for a number of other important reforms. With the abolition of serfdom the patrimonial jurisdiction and police authority which the landlords had exercised over their serfs disappeared automatically, and at the same time a blow was dealt to the prestige of the nobility in the country districts. A thorough reorganization of local government, up to this time entirely in the hands of the nobles, became imperative. In 1864 the so-called Zemstvo institutions were established in Russia. Three groups participated in the elections to the District Zemstvo Assembly: the private landowners, the peasant communes, and certain categories of the urban population. The District Zemstvo elected a permanent governing board and sent representatives to the Provincial Zemstvo, which in turn elected its own governing board. Both in the districts and in the provinces the Zemstvos concerned themselves with problems of public welfare, while general administrative functions and the exercise of police authority remained in the hands of crown officials. The Zemstvos in order to carry on their work were permitted to levy taxes for local needs. Their membership was elected on the basis of an unequal franchise, with the landowning nobility still occupying the most prominent place. Nevertheless, when compared with the situation before the reform this system was a decided step forward. The principle of self-government was openly recognized and an opportunity was given to various social classes to coöperate in improving local conditions. That this opportunity was not neglected is shown by the fact that during the period of their existence the Zemstvos performed a highly valuable work which greatly contributed to the economic and cultural progress of rural Russia.

Scarcely less important than these changes in local government was the reform of the law courts (1864). To appreciate its significance one has to take into account the conditions which existed in the first half of the nineteenth century. The old courts were among the worst features of pre-reform Russia. Based on class distinctions, the administration of justice was in the hands of ill-paid, badly-trained and frequently corrupt magistrates who were subservient to the authorities and to the wealthier classes. The hearings were secret and there were no lawyers to protect the interests of the defendant. The procedure was slow and costly in the extreme. The reform of 1864 proclaimed the principle of "laws equally just to all" and did away with class distinctions. The courts were made independent of the administration, the judges became irremovable and were properly remunerated. Trials were made public, the jury was introduced, and the Bar was established. The whole procedure, from the lowest courts to the highest, was thoroughly reorganized. From that time on Russia possessed a judicial system which could compare favorably with those of other civilized countries.

The last reform of major importance was the reorganization of the army (1874). Up to that time the whole burden of military conscription had rested on the lower classes of the population, who had to serve in the army for a very long period of time and under extremely harsh and exacting conditions. The reform of 1874 established universal military service.[1] The term of actual service was reduced from twenty-five to six years, and its conditions were improved to a very considerable extent. Treatment of soldiers became immeasurably more humane, the whole system of training was reorganized, and special attention began to be paid to the problem of gen-

[1] Universal military service, as used in the law of 1874, really meant universal obligation to serve if called. Exemptions were regularly granted to only sons and to others who were the sole support of their families. Educated persons enjoyed a greatly reduced term of service.

eral education in the ranks. Like the new courts, the new army was a symbol of Russia's modernization.

RUSSIA AFTER THE REFORMS

It is not difficult to see that all the major reforms of Alexander II tended in one direction, the breaking down of legal barriers which the old order had erected between the various classes. The abolition of serfdom did away with the fundamental distinction between those who were and those who were not personally free. In the Zemstvo assemblies the liberated serfs sat side by side with their former masters and were looked upon, at least theoretically, as equals of the representatives of other classes. The new courts introduced the ideal of "laws equally just to all" and as a rule adhered to this ideal in practice. And finally, the reorganized Russian army was based on the democratic principle of compulsory military service on the part of every citizen. It must be said, however, that even after the Emancipation the peasants did not become full-fledged citizens. As members of the village commune they could not dispose of their property and their freedom of movement was somewhat limited. For minor offenses they were tried by special courts on the basis of special laws. And the poll-tax, which they still had to pay and from which other classes were exempt, was a mark of their social inferiority. But even with these limitations, the general effect of the reforms was to bring Russia many steps nearer civil equality.

The same leveling process was at work in the field of economic and social relations. As a result of the Emancipation the nobility lost not only a considerable part of their land, but also their free supply of labor. Hindered by lack of initiative, of special training and of capital, many of the former serf-owners failed to adjust themselves to new conditions. There were many cases of downright bankruptcy, and still more numerous were the occasions when the owners of the estates preferred to sell their land rather than to struggle against adverse circumstances. The transfer of land from the nobles to the non-noble owners remained one of the outstanding phenomena in the economic life of Russia up to the end of the imperial régime. Together with the nobility's land ownership, the social hegemony of the nobles within the country was gradually passing away.

What was lost by the nobles was gained by other social classes. It was only after the Emancipation that there began in Russia that advance of the middle classes which had been going on in western Europe for centuries. The accelerated development of industry, to which more attention will be paid in another section, resulted in the growth of a bourgeoisie; wealth other than in land began to serve as a foundation for high social position. Growth of trade made the merchant class more numerous and more important and there was a noticeable effort on the part of many merchants to rise above their former social and cultural standards. The reforms, moreover, opened new fields of activity which did not exist before. Work in the Zemstvos and in the new courts, even in some of the governmental departments, began to attract many public-spirited men who under the old order would have shunned governmental service and condemned themselves to inactivity. Economic progress called for an increasing number of technical specialists; the growing demand for popular education and a general intellectual awakening were responsible for a notable increase in the numbers of teachers, writers, and journalists. For the first time in Russian history the doctor, the lawyer, the university professor, the engineer, were coming to the forefront as important and influential members of society. One may say that a new class, that of the professional men, made its appearance in Russia.

By all these changes the Russian *intelligentsia* [1] which had been formed in the preceding period was greatly affected. Confined in the beginning to the progressive members of the nobility, the ranks of the *intelligentsia* were now rapidly increased by professional men and representatives of the middle classes in general. No longer were the enlightened noblemen the standard-bearers of education and progress. Their place was being taken by the middle class intellectuals, who as a rule were less refined in their culture and more radical in their social and political views. It was only with the appearance of the middle-class element that the *intelligentsia* acquired a definite group-consciousness and became the backbone of the political opposition.

In no other field was the advance of the middle classes so pronounced as in that of education. The reforms played the part of a powerful stimulant to the intellectual life of the country; there was a widespread and incessantly growing demand for knowledge on the part of practically all groups of the population. Throughout the second half of the nineteenth century one can observe a steady progress both with regard to the universities and the secondary schools; moreover, it was in this period that, thanks to the active participation of the Zemstvos, a real start was made in the field of primary education. The number of schools not only increased, but the distribution of students between the various social classes also underwent a significant change. In this field as in

[1] The word *"intelligentsia"* is used in this study in a limited sense, to designate the politically-minded part of the educated class in opposition to the government.

others the nobility was gradually losing its former predominance; by the end of the period students of noble origin represented but a minority both in the universities and the secondary schools. As for governmental policy, it remained, as before, self-contradictory, fluctuating between a fairly liberal stand at one time and a decidedly reactionary one at another. But no artificial obstacles could effectively block the cultural progress of the middle classes and, to a lesser extent, even that of the peasantry. The development which was taking place in the schools was but a reflection of the general trend of social evolution within the country. Beginning with the period of the reforms a democratic society was growing in Russia under an autocratic government.

THE CREED OF THE "INTELLIGENTSIA"

The new social groups that became predominant in the ranks of the *intelligentsia* brought with them new ideas. The outstanding Russian intellectuals of the preceding period were romanticists and idealists, brought up in the school of German metaphysics and deeply interested in philosophy, poetry, and art. Even when they became engaged in a discussion of political and social problems, their politics retained a broadly philosophical character. The new generation that took the place of these early intellectuals was of a widely different nature. They liked to call themselves "critical realists." They had no use for metaphysics, and professed indifference to the esthetic side of life. For them the universe was "not a temple, but a workshop," and they aspired to be artisans of progress with scientific knowledge as their tool. This positivist reaction against the romantic idealism of the earlier generation was one of the outstanding features of the movement known as "Nihilism" which took place in the sixties. Nihilism was primarily a revolt of youth against traditional authority; it had for its chief purpose the liberation of the individual from all established conventions. Nothing was sacred to the Nihilists (hence their very name); nothing was to be accepted as valid unless it could stand the test of rational criticism. Emancipation of woman was one of their favorite battle-cries and, as a matter of fact, the Russian girl of the educated class became emancipated long before her west-European or even her American sisters. Although Nihilism as such was devoid of a definite political character, this general defiance of authority could not fail to produce a revolutionizing effect.

The real social movement came forward in the next decade with so-called "Populism." In contradistinction to the Nihilists, the Populists were interested not in the emancipation of the individual but in finding a solution for the social problem. The dominating idea of Populism was that of the moral duty on the part of the *intelligentsia* to serve the "people," identified in practice with the peasantry. For centuries the educated class of Russia had been living and developing at the expense of peasant suffering; now was the time to repay the debt. The intellectuals had to "go to the people," to live and to work among the peasants and to lead the latter along the path of cultural and social progress. In the early seventies young men and young girls of the educated class began by hundreds to take up different positions in the villages in order to fulfill this obligation. The movement was remarkable for its crusading spirit, but also for its lack of practical preparation and its feebly developed sense of reality.

Both Nihilism and Populism were extreme manifestations of the new intellectual tendencies among the young

Russian radicals, but many of their fundamental tenets became widely accepted by the *intelligentsia* as a whole and were destined to dominate the educated class of the country for a long time. One may say that throughout the second half of the nineteenth century the majority of Russian intellectuals remained socially- and politically-minded almost to the complete exclusion of any other spiritual interest. The idea of civic duty reigned supreme. Art for art's sake became a dangerous heresy, and all artistic activity had to be subordinated to demands of a utilitarian nature. Generally speaking, the age of poetry was over and the ideal of truth was boldly substituted for that of beauty not only in literature, but also in painting and, in some cases, even in music. Criticism became political and social, rather than literary or artistic. A novel, a picture, a play, or a poem was hailed or voted down not on its proper merits but because it was progressive or reactionary, as the case might be. A typical member of the *intelligentsia* was either indifferent or openly hostile towards religion and tended to be profoundly suspicious of every idealistic interpretation of the universe. As always there were some notable exceptions; giants like Tolstoi and Dostoevski could go their own way without impairing thereby their popularity. But what was permitted to a genius was not forgiven in the case of a lesser man. As a rule the *intelligentsia* was intolerant and uncompromising in its attitude toward the dissenters.

THE REVOLUTIONARY MOVEMENT UNDER ALEXANDER II

It may seem at first puzzling that the reforms of Alexander II, far-reaching as they were, failed to satisfy the progressive groups of Russian society and that the first two decades after the Emancipation saw the growth in Russia of a political opposition which was far more outspoken and determined than it ever had been before. To say that this opposition was entirely provoked by governmental reaction would be hardly correct: the first revolutionary proclamations, calling for a bitter struggle against the government, appeared as early as 1861-62, when the reform movement was still at its height; the first attempt against the emperor's life took place in 1866, only five years after the Emancipation. The revival of the political opposition should be ascribed rather to that general atmosphere of change and renovation which the Great Reforms brought into Russian life. As in the early days of Alexander I, the reformist policies of the government again played the part of a powerful stimulus for the development of advanced political and social ideas among the educated classes of the Russian people and, as before, progressive public opinion moved ahead of the government. To the reforms that had been granted the opposition answered with a demand for more reforms.

For the liberals [1] the abolition of serfdom and the introduction of local self-government was but a prelude to what they called "the crowning of the building," the establishment in Russia of a system of national representation. Some of the constitutional projects of the period emanated from the nobility who desired political gains as compensation for their economic losses under the Emancipation settlement. Other projects were of a more unselfish origin and were dictated by a theoretical predilection for constitutional government. The radicals went much further than the liberals. What they wanted was not to substitute a parliamentary régime for autoc-

---

[1] The words "liberalism" and "liberal" are used in this study in their European sense, namely, to designate the party of moderate and peaceful reform as distinguished from the revolutionary socialists.

racy, but to bring about a complete destruction of the old social order.

From the outset the revolutionary movement of the sixties and the seventies was completely dominated by the socialists. It was during these decades that Russian socialism acquired both a definite doctrine and a fighting organization. Both in theory and in practice it differed considerably from the west-European socialism of the same period. It was based not on the teachings of Karl Marx but on the ideas of Russian writers such as Herzen and Chernyshevski. It shared the Slavophils' belief in the peculiarities of Russia's historical development and it looked upon the Russian peasant, living in his village commune, as a socialist by instinct and tradition, whose mission it was to save Russia from capitalism and to bring her directly into the communist era. Partly because of this theory and partly because of the fact that Russian capitalism still was in the first stages of development, the early Russian socialists, with few exceptions, were much more interested in the peasantry than in the industrial workers. Their socialism, in other words, had an agrarian character. Another fundamental feature that distinguished the majority of Russian socialists of the period was their complete distrust of parliamentary democracy, which in their eyes had no value whatsoever even as an intermediary stage of development. What they wanted was a more or less immediate social revolution and not a gradual approach to socialism by the long way of evolution.

At first, however, there was no unanimity of views as to the proper means to bring about the revolution. Some admitted the necessity of a preliminary period of propaganda to educate and organize the peasantry, while others were confident of their ability to stir up a general peasant uprising without much preparation. Both methods were tried by those who "went to the people," but neither proved to be a success. The propagandists were not understood by the peasants and at the same time were easily detected by the police, while the revolutionary appeals of the more impatient among the Populists failed to provoke a general insurrection. It was then that the idea of a direct attack upon the government, led by an organized minority, took hold of the minds of the majority of Russian radicals. At the time when west-European socialism was beginning to ally itself with mass movement, as expressed either in trade-unions or in political labor parties, the Russian socialists saw themselves forced to choose the narrow and perilous path of revolutionary conspiracy.

The prevalence of this tendency among the radical groups of the *intelligentsia* was due in no small measure to the policy of the government. The liberal ardor of Alexander's early years was all but spent in the strenuous effort to carry through the abolition of serfdom. This and other reforms met with a tremendous opposition on the part of those reactionaries who never become reconciled to the new order of things. Throughout the reign of Alexander II they continued to struggle with the more liberal elements for predominance in governmental councils, with the easily influenced emperor vacillating between the two mutually exclusive policies. The enemies of the reforms skillfully used every opportunity to strengthen their position with the sovereign. Events like the Polish insurrection of 1863 and the first attempt upon Alexander's life in 1866 were interpreted as indicating the danger of concessions and the necessity of a sterner policy. With the growth of the revolutionary movement these arguments acquired a more telling effect: in order to combat radicalism it was deemed necessary to curtail the reforms that had been granted. Censorship was again strengthened and freedom of teaching limited. Press cases and political offenses were exempt from trial by jury. Side by side with the regular court procedure there was gradually set up an elaborate system of exceptional jurisdiction under which offenders were dealt with either by military tribunals or by means of mere administrative orders. The Zemstvos were subject to strict governmental supervision and their activities were constantly interfered with by local authorities. Above all, a firm resistance was offered to any suggestions favoring the limitation of autocracy and the extension of the principle of self-government to the management of national affairs.

The reaction was not able to nullify the effects of the reforms and to restore the old order of things, but it greatly impeded Russia's progress, and, by generating bitterness and distrust, made extremely difficult a peaceful solution of the country's outstanding problems. One of the worst features of this policy was its failure to discriminate between the radical aspirations of the revolutionaries and the more moderate demands of the constitutionalists. With a few notable exceptions the rulers of Russia were unable to appreciate the wisdom of a policy that would combat revolution by reform. An attempt of this kind was made in the last years of Alexander's reign by his Minister of the Interior Loris-Melikov, a wise and able statesman, who, while fully determined to stamp out revolutionary activities, was nevertheless prepared to satisfy some of the desires of the progressive groups of Russian society. He finally succeeded in persuading the emperor to approve his project (sometimes erroneously referred to as a "constitution") of inviting representatives of public bodies to coöperate with the government in working out a program of further reforms. His attempt was frustrated by the assassination of Alexander II by the revolutionaries in March, 1881.

This tragic event was the outcome of the desperate struggle which a small band of determined revolutionaries waged against the government during the last years of Alexander's reign. In 1879 the revolutionaries became organized under the name of the "Will of the People." It was a highly centralized and secret body, with terrorism as its chief weapon. Assassination of several prominent officials was followed by a series of daring attempts upon the life of the emperor. Although the efforts of the terrorists were finally crowned with success, the whole movement must be considered as politically futile. It is significant only because it reveals the character and mutual relations of the main forces involved in the struggle. On the one hand we see the uncompromising and stubborn autocracy, on the other equally uncompromising and stubborn revolutionaries. Caught between the two fires were the advocates of a middle course, the Russian liberals who, while the radicals were throwing bombs to which the government answered by executions, confined themselves to voicing their demands and offering counsels of moderation. The tragedy of the constitutional movement in Russia lay in the fact that it represented middle class liberalism without a sufficiently active and numerous middle class from which to recruit its strength. Deprived of an adequate social base of its own, it could not ally itself wholeheartedly with either of the two extremes and so was doomed to fail in its efforts to bring about a peaceful regeneration of the country.

Alexander III (1881-1894) was profoundly influenced by the circumstances of his accession. A staunch conservative, he had consistently sided with the reactionaries against the liberals while still heir to the throne. The assassination of his father confirmed him in this attitude. Here was a direct attack on the sovereign power, led by forces of destruction, which had to be repulsed and suppressed without mercy. It was under the influence of this tragic event that Alexander III decided to discard the Loris-Melikov project, already approved by his father but unpublished. A manifesto of the new emperor announced to the Russian people his firm intention to "strengthen and guard the autocracy from any possible encroachments." After a brief period of hesitation and uncertainty, during which some of the reforming tendencies of the previous reign were still permitted to exist, the government of Alexander III finally started upon the road of complete political reaction. This reactionary course was pursued until the end of the reign and was bequeathed by Alexander III to his son and successor, Nicholas II.

To a very considerable extent this policy was shaped and inspired by a man whose very name became a symbol of reaction, Constantin Pobedonostsev. A former professor of civil law in the University of Moscow, Pobedonostsev had been Alexander's tutor since the latter's early youth and had gained an undisputed ascendancy over the mind of his royal pupil. As Procurator of the Holy Synod he was now one of the most influential members of the government and he remained in this position throughout the reign of Alexander III and the early part of that of Nicholas II. Pobedonostsev was more than a mere reactionary statesman; he was a philosopher of reaction. In ringing terms he denounced parliamentary democracy, freedom of the press, separation of church and state, and even universal education as great fallacies of modern times working for the destruction of all that was vigorous and healthy in a nation. From these unmitigated evils he wanted to save Russia at any cost. Under his influence the old formula "Orthodoxy, Autocracy, Nationalism" was revived and given new strength in its practical applications. Not only was the revolutionary movement stamped out for the time being, but even moderate liberals were sternly rebuked and silenced. Censorship was again strengthened and freedom of teaching was further curtailed. The laws concerning local self-government were revised and the Zemstvos became subject to much stricter governmental supervision. Simultaneously, the representation of the nobility in the Zemstvo assemblies was considerably increased at the expense of other classes. The nobility once more became a favorite with the crown. The idea was that the nobles represented the natural mainstay of autocracy and as such should be helped to regain their predominant position. Among other things the nobles were called upon to assist the government in exercising paternalistic control over the peasantry. In 1889 the office of "land captain" was created. These "land captains" were local officials appointed by the government from among the landowning nobility to exercise administrative power and even to a certain extent judicial authority over the peasants in the country districts.

The support of orthodoxy was expressed in a policy of persecution of religious dissenters, the so-called "old believers" and the sectarians.[1] Some of these were practically denied any legal status and were accordingly driven underground. The position of the Roman Catholics and the Lutherans (the most numerous of the Protestant denominations in Russia), however, was considerably better. They were legally recognized as religious bodies, having their separate church organizations and owning property. But even they were discriminated against. To try to convert a Greek Orthodox into a Roman Catholic or a Lutheran was a crime punishable under the law, while it was equally a crime to try to prevent a Roman Catholic or a Lutheran from becoming a Greek Orthodox. In cases of mixed marriages children automatically became Greek Orthodox irrespective of their parents' wishes.

The policy of the government in support of the domination of the Greek Orthodox Church found a counterpart in its attitude towards the national minorities. Here the slogan was "Russia for the true Russians." Those of the supposedly pure Great Russian origin had to be given preference over the White Russians and the Ukrainians, not to speak of the representatives of alien races. In the border provinces "Russification" became the order of the day. Efforts were made to force the non-Russian inhabitants of these regions to give up their own national traditions and to recognize the superiority of Russian culture. This policy was pursued with particular stubbornness with regard to Poland which had lost, after the sup-

---

[1] The "old believers" were a group that split off from the Greek Orthodox Church in the latter part of the seventeenth century. They differed from the official church in questions of ritual only. On the other hand, the sectarians, such as the Dukhobors and the Molokans, followed religious doctrines that were fundamentally different from those of the Greek Orthodox Church.

pression of the insurrection of 1863, the last remnants of its former autonomy. Even the German barons of the Baltic provinces, who for generations had been loyal subjects of the Russian monarchy, now were also discriminated against, although in a somewhat milder fashion. The chief sufferers of all, however, were the Jews. Since the beginning of the nineteenth century the majority of them had been kept within a certain restricted area known as the "Jewish pale." Under Alexander III the boundaries of the "pale" were narrowed and the prohibition against living outside the "pale" was strictly enforced. The civil rights of the Jews were subject to many obnoxious restrictions and only a limited number of Jewish youths were permitted to enter the schools and the universities.

From the historical point of view the reactionary policy of Alexander III represented a hopeless anachronism. It was an attempt to restore a past that was dead beyond any possibility of resurrection. To base the governmental policy on an alliance between autocracy and nobility was to ignore the whole trend of Russia's social evolution since the Emancipation. With the abolition of serfdom the very basis of the nobility's power and influence was irreparably destroyed. Neither economically, nor socially, nor intellectually were the nobles any longer in a position to dominate the country to the exclusion of other classes. No less unfortunate than this alliance with the nobility was the tendency to replace the broad conception of the Empire as a political structure sheltering many races and nationalities by a rigid formula of exclusive nationalism, reposing on a narrow ethnical basis. This was a decided step backward if compared with the more cosmopolitan outlook of the imperial government in the days of Catherine II or in the early part of the nineteenth century. It was a symptom of a mortal disease: the Russian autocracy was doomed to speedy decay, and while approaching the end it was losing its imperial consciousness.

THE INDUSTRIAL REVOLUTION

It has already been shown that early in the nineteenth century capitalistic tendencies became clearly discernible in the economic life of Russia. Yet so long as Russia's national economy remained dominated by serfdom, these tendencies could not develop to the utmost of their possibilities. In this respect, too, the Emancipation was the turning point. After a certain period of inevitable confusion, during which the economic life of the country tried to adjust itself to new conditions, there began that process of accelerated industrial progress along capitalistic lines which might be designated as the coming into Russia of the Industrial Revolution. The period saw the rapid development of those technical means without which no real capitalistic advance was possible. Extensive railroad building was one of the outstanding features of Russian life in the latter part of the nineteenth century. At first concessions for the construction of railroad lines were granted by the government to private companies. As a rule, however, these proved to be rather inefficient and their activities were accompanied by all kinds of questionable financial transactions. With characteristic paternalism the government soon decided to take matters into its own hands. A number of private railroads were purchased by the Treasury and new lines were built and operated directly by the government. State railroads finally became the predominant type in Russia, while those private lines that were permitted to exist were subject to a rather strict governmental control. By the end of the nineteenth century Russia was adding to her rail-

way mileage more rapidly than any other country in
Europe. If the development of her railroad system still
lagged behind the needs of the country, this was due
partly to the fact that she had started extensive railroad
building rather late and, even more, to the enormous size
of her territory.

Another problem of great importance was that of credit
facilities. Prior to the reform period Russia had practically no credit system worthy of the name. It was only
after the Emancipation that modern banking began to develop in the country. Here, of course, private initiative
had to play the most important part. But even in this
field the participation of the government was far more
active than in the capitalist countries of western Europe.
Besides the State Bank of the usual type the Russian government established some special credit institutions of its
own. Finally, one of the chief concerns of the government
during the decades in question was the improvement of
the monetary situation. Since the Crimean War Russia
had been living under a most unsatisfactory régime of
depreciated paper currency. From 1862 on a number of
fairly able ministers of finance attempted to establish the
gold standard by gradually increasing the Treasury's reserve. But it was not until 1897 that this attempt proved
successful. The effect of this monetary reform upon Russia's economic progress hardly needs to be emphasized.
Not only did it create conditions of stability for commercial operations within the country, but by putting Russian
currency on a basis of parity with those of other countries it also made possible a very considerable influx of
foreign capital into Russia in the form of loans and in-
vestments.

Closely connected with railroad building and financial
reforms was the rapid industrial development of the coun-

try. Striking progress was achieved in the metallurgical industry, greatly stimulated by the discovery of vast deposits of coal and iron in South Russia. Another branch of industry which, towards the end of the century, showed remarkable progress was the manufacture of textiles, particularly in Central Russia. Trade grew with industry and there was a significant increase in the number of joint-stock companies, a comparatively recent phenomenon in Russian economic life.

No other single man among the Russian statesmen of the period was so closely connected with the industrial revolution as was Witte, Minister of Finance from 1892 to 1903. If Pobedonostsev was a symbol of political reaction, Witte's name stood for economic progress. Far from being a liberal, he was a splendid opportunist, a business man in politics, and a "modern" in his general outlook and methods. Devoid of any personal charm and not always able to inspire confidence in those around him, he must be given credit for the magnitude of his schemes and the technical skill he displayed in their execution. It was Witte who finally carried through the monetary reform in spite of strong opposition and it was he again who for some time actually directed railroad building in Russia, being largely responsible among other things for the construction of the great Trans-Siberian railroad in 1892-1904. A firm believer in industrialization and with an ideal of an economically self-dependent Russia before his eyes, Witte spared no effort to support the development of Russian industry by a policy of tariff protection, governmental guarantees, and subsidies.

One of the inevitable results of the Industrial Revolution was the growth in Russia of a city proletariat. For the first time in Russian history the government had to face the labor problem in its modern aspects. During

this early period of the capitalistic advance labor conditions in Russia were particularly unsatisfactory, as they
had been to a greater or less degree in other countries
during similar economic transformations. Because of the
general backwardness of the country, which but yesterday
had emerged from serfdom, these conditions were probably several degrees worse in Russia than they had been
anywhere else. As a rule the factory hands were over-
worked, underpaid, and badly fed and lodged. To the
ruthless exploitation of their labor by the pioneers of
Russian capitalism the workers answered with sporadic
outbursts of discontent and poorly organized strikes.
The government felt that it must interfere and try to improve the situation. The years 1882-1886 saw the real
beginning of labor legislation in Russia. Although rather
modest in scope and dealing chiefly with the protection
of women and children, these early factory laws represented a creditable start in the right direction. A decade
later (1897) they were supplemented by a law which limited day work of adults to eleven and a half hours and
night work to ten hours. To ensure the observance of
these laws the office of factory inspector was established.
The work of these inspectors, however, was not always
sufficient to overcome the stubborn opposition on the part
of many employers. Furthermore, the situation was ag-
gravated by the fact that until 1902 no trade-unions were
permitted by the government to exist. No wonder that
under such limitations the improvement in labor conditions was neither rapid nor substantial enough to prevent
the growth of discontent among the working masses of
the cities.

THE AGRARIAN CRISIS

While Russian industry was making rapid and in some
respects spectacular progress, Russian agriculture was

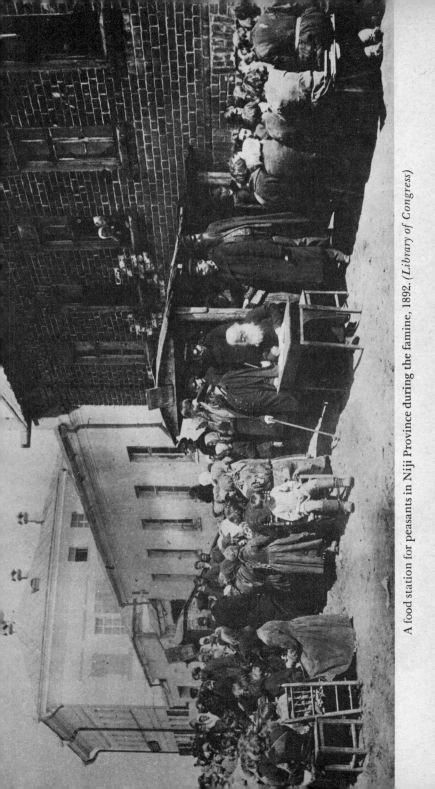

A food station for peasants in Niji Province during the famine, 1892. (*Library of Congress*)

A southern Russian and his wife, 1888. *(Library of Congress)*

passing through a prolonged crisis. As far as large-scale farming was concerned, this crisis was partly due to the general depression from which European agriculture was suffering during the last decades of the nineteenth century as a result of the growing competition on the part of non-European countries. In Russia there was an additional factor: the extremely difficult situation in which many landlords found themselves after the Emancipation. As has been indicated above, perhaps the majority of the former serf-owners possessed neither capital nor the initiative which would permit them to adjust themselves immediately to new conditions. On the other hand, even with the credit facilities which they could obtain from the special Land Bank established for them by the government, many nobles failed to use this assistance to the best advantage. Thus a long period of time had to pass before there could arise in Russia a new type of large landowner, able to organize his farming along capitalistic lines.

But the gravest problem was the plight of the peasant. Although conditions differed in various localities and among various groups of the peasantry, there can be no doubt that the situation in which the peasants found themselves towards the end of the nineteenth century was on the whole most unsatisfactory. Particularly ominous was the fact that a large part of the Russian people were living in poverty and were not always able to earn subsistence for themselves or to discharge their obligations towards the state. At times, as during the severe famine of 1891-93, conditions became almost catastrophic, but even in the periods of good harvests the standard of living in the villages remained in most cases extremely low.

In the discussion of the Russian agrarian problem two factors have usually been given prominence as causes of the impoverishment of the peasantry: the insufficiency of land allotments received by the peasants at the Emancipation, and the amount of redemption payments, which, combined with taxes, constituted too heavy a burden for them to carry. While it is not possible to deny the highly unfavorable influence of these factors, one should be careful not to overemphasize their importance. It is in the general economic conditions within the country that one has to look for the principal cause of the crisis. The whole situation can be summarized as a case of agrarian over-population. The chief trouble was that while the rural population was growing very rapidly, there was very little progress in agricultural technique, the land was not used to the best advantage, and the yield of peasant farming remained miserably low. At the same time the relatively tardy industrialization of the country made it impossible for the factories to absorb the excess labor in the countryside. Nor was large scale capitalistic farming sufficiently developed to provide these workers with employment. As a result, the majority of the peasants remained congested in the agricultural regions of central Russia without any real possibility of improving their conditions. In the eyes of the peasants, the only remedy for their ills was to obtain more land. This they were trying to do both by buying and leasing land from the landlords. But as the methods of cultivation remained as backward as before, such an extension of peasant holdings failed to bring about any substantial improvement while it added, particularly in the case of rented land, to the financial burden which the peasantry had to carry.

Still another factor has to be taken into consideration: the then prevailing type of peasant tenure in Russia. The village commune directly interfered with the general economic progress of the countryside. By its open-field system, in which the individual holdings of the peasants were divided into widely-scattered strips, and by its periodical redistributions of land, the commune thwarted personal initiative and introduced an element of instability that was bound to react most unfavorably on all attempts at technical improvement. At the same time, because of the joint liability for the payment of redemption installments and taxes, the commune interfered with the freedom of movement among the rural population of Russia. In this way it hindered the natural process of social differentiation in the villages and artificially kept in the overcrowded rural districts many of those peasants who otherwise would have severed their connection with the land and would have looked for occupation elsewhere.

It would be unfair to say that the Russian government of the period neglected the plight of the peasants. Several important measures were passed under Alexander III which attempted to meet the agrarian crisis and to improve the conditions of the peasantry. In 1881 the redemption payments were reduced almost twenty-seven per cent; five years later the poll tax was abolished. A Peasant Land Bank was established in 1882 to grant the peasants credit for buying land, but the activities of the Bank did not acquire real importance until after 1905. Finally, peasant migration to Asiatic Russia was stimulated by a policy of organized governmental assistance which, however, remained comparatively ineffective until the construction of the Trans-Siberian railroad.

Important as all these measures were, they were not sufficient to solve the peasant problem. Partly because the governmental policy still lacked necessary vigor and consistency, but chiefly on account of the general economic situation, the agrarian crisis continued unabated and "land hunger" remained the most powerful motive in the class psychology of the Russian peasants.

THE LIBERATION MOVEMENT AND THE RUSSO-JAPANESE WAR

During the reign of Alexander III political discontent and social unrest were largely kept underground. But the accession of Nicholas II (1894-1917) opened a new period in the history of the Russian revolutionary movement. The new sovereign, whose fate it was to become the last of the Romanovs, assumed his duties with an intention "to maintain the principle of autocracy as firmly and unswervingly as it was by his lamented father." The reactionary policy of Alexander III was followed in practically every direction; in some respects it was even intensified. Thus, for instance, the first serious attempt was made to violate the autonomy of Finland, which up to that time had managed to preserve its privileges more or less unmolested. The Zemstvo representatives who, upon the accession of the new emperor, dared to express in a most loyal manner their hope for a more liberal policy, were sternly rebuked for these "senseless dreams" of theirs. Pobedonostsev's influence remained supreme and other staunch reactionaries continued to occupy the most important posts in the administration. Very soon, however, it became clear that the government was no longer able to prevent the outbursts of political discontent by mere repression and that forces of opposition were growing within the country over which the autocracy was gradually losing its control. From the late nineties the opposition began to assume a more widespread and at the same time an increasingly radical character, until it culminated in 1905 in an open and partially victorious conflict with the government.

This "liberation movement," as it is known in Russian historiography, differed substantially from the earlier phase of the revolutionary development. Due to the general democratization of Russian society that had been going on since the reforms of Alexander II, and also as a result of the Industrial Revolution, the opposition now acquired a much wider social basis than it had ever possessed before. It was also much better organized and it worked out a more definite program. One of the fateful events of the period was the appearance in Russia of Marxian socialism, with its emphasis on the revolutionary mission of the industrial proletariat and the primary importance of the class struggle. In the growing class of factory workers, dissatisfied with labor conditions, the Russian followers of Karl Marx found a fertile soil for their propaganda. In 1898 there was organized a Russian Social-Democratic party (S.D.'s in abbreviation) which several years later split into two factions, one headed by Plekhanov and the other by Lenin. The former, called the Mensheviks, expected the forthcoming Russian revolution to be of a "bourgeois" character, which would bring about the establishment in Russia of a political democracy as a preliminary step on the way to socialism. The latter, the Bolsheviks, insisted on the necessity of proceeding directly from the overthrow of autocracy to the complete realization of the socialist ideal. Another socialist party which was organized about the same time and which took the name of Socialist Revolutionaries (S.R.'s in abbreviation) revived the agrarian tradition of the Populists by concentrating its attention on the peasantry. With its slogan "All land to the working people" it found a ready response on the part of the peasants suffering from "land hunger." In their tactics the S.R.'s also followed the example of the earlier Russian revolutionaries by choosing terrorism as one of their

chief weapons, with the result that a series of assassinations of unpopular officials took place.   While both the
S.D.'s and the S.R.'s were able to win a considerable
popular following, the leadership remained in the hands
of the intellectuals: active members were still chiefly recruited from the enthusiastic youth of the educated class.
One of the most characteristic features of the Russian
revolutionary movement was the great part played in it
by university students.   Again and again the normal
academic life of the universities was interrupted by students' political strikes and demonstrations.

   Paralleling the growth of socialist parties was the
development of a liberal movement aiming at the establishment in Russia of a representative government and a
constitutional régime.   From the beginning Russian liberalism found refuge in the Zemstvo assemblies.   The
government tried hard to keep the Zemstvos within the
narrow limits of non-political local activities but, in spite
of this, the progressive elements among the Zemstvo
workers were inevitably becoming more and more involved in national politics.   In the absence of any parliamentary institutions the Zemstvos played the part of
a school of self-government.   By the end of the nineteenth
century, however, liberalism was able to find many re-
cruits among the professional groups which had been
steadily growing since the Emancipation.   It was the
combination of these two elements—the Zemstvo workers and the members of liberal professions—which brought
about the formation in 1903 of the so-called "Union of
Liberation."   Guided by such men as Struve and Miliukov, both of them outstanding scholars and writers, and
counting in its ranks some of the finest intellects in the
country, the "Union of Liberation" assumed for a while
a leading part in the opposition movement to which it

gave its name. It served also eventually as a nucleus for the Constitutional Democratic party, popularly known as the Cadets.

The liberation movement was already well on its way when Russia became involved in a new war. This war was an outcome of Russia's expansion in the Far East, which brought her into a conflict with the expanding power of Japan. It is doubtful, however, whether an armed conflict between the two nations was absolutely inevitable. In approaching the problem one must distinguish between the vital and legitimate interests of Russia, on the one hand, and the imperialistic policy of the Russian autocracy, on the other. Russia's expansion towards the Pacific, the beginnings of which go back to the sixteenth century, if not earlier, was an elemental movement on the part of the Russian people and not a case of an organized governmental conquest. The whole of Siberia had been gradually acquired and settled by a process of pioneering and colonization which bore rather striking resemblance to the gradual "winning of the West" by the American people. The construction of the Trans-Siberian railroad was designed primarily to facilitate this process of settlement by bringing Siberia into a closer union with the mother country, as well as to provide a commercial outlet for the growing economic activity of the eastern part of the Empire. Under an agreement concluded between Russia and China in 1896, part of the railroad was laid across Chinese territory, running through Northern Manchuria and thus greatly shortening the line which otherwise would have had to follow the very prominent curve formed by the political boundary. Although China ceded to Russia for the term of the concession sovereign rights within the railway zone, this arrangement in itself was no more objectionable than similar arrangements connected with the Panama and the Suez canals. As was inevitable under such circumstances, the Chinese Eastern railroad, as it was called, became an instrument of Russia's economic influence in Manchuria. This policy, however, could have remained a rather mild form of imperialism, of the "peaceful penetration" brand, and it did not necessarily preclude the possibility of an understanding with Japan. What did preclude this possibility was the series of acts that followed: the seizure of Port Arthur on the Liaotung Peninsula (1898), the prolonged military occupation of Manchuria after the suppression of the Boxer Rebellion (1900), and, above all, political intrigues in Korea, led by a group of irresponsible adventurers who unfortunately had gained influence at the Russian court. It was this outburst of open aggressiveness that greatly antagonized both China and Japan, raised grave suspicions on the part of other foreign powers, obscured the real nature of Russia's national interests in the Far East, and served as a direct cause of the Russo-Japanese War (1904-1905).

It is hardly necessary to re-tell the familiar story of the war which ended in the dramatically unexpected defeat of Russia by the Japanese. Several factors of primary importance contributed to this result. Japan had her base close to the field of operations, while Russia's was separated from it by an enormous distance with one single-track railroad to rely upon for transportation of troops and supplies. Japan began the war fully prepared, while Russia, in spite of her aggressive policy, was caught unawares. Above all, the war was one of national defense for the Japanese, while the Russian people remained indifferent to the issues involved or even hostile towards the imperialistic policy of the government.

In the political history of Russia the conflict with

Japan played a part strikingly similar to that of the Crimean War. Again the conduct of military operations revealed all the fundamental weaknesses and defects of the existing system. Again the humiliation of defeat added fuel to the political discontent that had been accumulating for some time. And again an unsuccessful war opened a new period in the internal development of the country. Expert opinion differs as to what extent the Japanese victory was a decisive one. But in the last stages of the struggle military considerations became for Russia of a secondary importance. Peace had to be concluded because in the summer of 1905 the country was already in the throes of a revolution.

CHAPTER III

THE CONSTITUTIONAL EXPERIMENT
(1905-1917)

THE REVOLUTION OF 1905

THE revolution of 1905 did not result in the destruction of the old social order desired by the radicals, nor did it bring about a complete realization of the more moderate demands of the constitutionalists. Yet its effects were far-reaching enough to permit us to consider it as beginning a new period in Russian history. In no less degree than the reforms of Alexander II, it modified the whole life of the nation and opened the way to new and significant developments.

During the first period of the revolution the Russian autocracy had to face a formidable coalition of all the forces of opposition within the country. For the time being the liberal constitutionalists and the radical socialists were acting in common. Late in 1904, after the assassination of the Minister of the Interior Plehve, the government first relaxed its policy of suppression; the Zemstvo conferences became instrumental in formulating the immediate demands of the opposition: convocation of a representative assembly and the grant to the Russian people of civil liberties guaranteed by a constitution. The Zemstvo program was immediately taken up by various professional groups at a series of political banquets held all over Russia during the winter of 1904-1905. A number of professional unions, organized for obviously political purposes, were finally merged into an impressive Union of Unions, headed by Miliukov, the recognized leader of the constitutionalists. While this organization of liberal forces was going on in the open, the socialists intensified their underground activities. The Social Revolutionaries were responsible for several dramatic assassinations of prominent reactionary officials and, at the same time, applied themselves to the task of stirring up rebellion among the discontented peasants of the rural districts. The Social Democrats, on the other hand, concentrated their attention on the industrial workers of the cities whom they tried to win over to their revolutionary program. Their task was greatly facilitated by the events of January 9, 1905, when a procession of St. Petersburg workers, headed for the imperial residence to present their grievances to the Tsar, was fired upon by the troops, and many workers killed or wounded. The effect of "Bloody Sunday" was to intensify the radicalism of the working masses and, during the spring and summer of 1905, all the industrial regions of Russia saw a veritable epidemic of strikes, which almost completely disorganized production. Simultaneously, spurred by revolutionary propaganda, the "land-hungry" peasants rose in many provinces of European Russia, burning and looting the neighboring estates and occasionally murdering the landlords.

Another important factor in the situation was the revolutionary movement among the national minorities of the border regions. Bitterly resenting the policy of enforced "Russification" which had been applied to them by the government during the previous decades, the Poles, the Jews, and the inhabitants of the Baltic provinces and of Transcaucasia, all joined hands with the Russian revolutionaries for a struggle against the common enemy. It must be said, however, that as yet this was not a separatist movement. In most cases the demands of the national minorities did not go beyond a program of equal rights and local autonomy. What they wanted was not to secede from the Empire, but to see it reorganized on a democratic and federalist basis.

Faced with this formidable array of hostile forces, the government found itself in an extremely difficult position. Engaged in a disastrously unsuccessful war, materially disorganized, and morally isolated, it tried for a while to save the situation with minor concessions. It was forced to admit defeat, however, when confronted, in October, 1905, by an unusually effective general strike, which for a few days almost paralyzed the whole life of the country. In this emergency Nicholas II turned for advice to Witte. With characteristic realism this experienced statesman offered his sovereign one of two alternatives: either to establish a military dictatorship or else, if this was not feasible, to grant the people a constitution. With the bulk of the army still in the Far East and the spirit of the immediately available troops rather uncertain (there were isolated revolutionary outbreaks both in the army and in the navy), the emperor reluctantly chose the latter of these suggestions.

A manifesto of October 17, 1905, granted the Russian people civil liberties and a representative legislative assembly, based on a democratic franchise. There could be no doubt as to the meaning of this pronouncement. Although not using the word, it contained a definite and solemn promise of a constitution. The publication of the manifesto was met with almost general rejoicing throughout Russia and it was hailed by the opposition as a real victory. Subsequent events showed, however, that Russia's troubles were not over and that the governmental concession, important as it was, failed to stop the revolutionary movement at once. The socialists were still bent upon the realization of their radical program, insisting on the complete abolition of monarchy, the establishment in Russia of a democratic republic, nationalization of land and other equally far-reaching social reforms. Under the leadership of the Soviet (Council) of Workers' Deputies, organized in St. Petersburg, strikes went on, and an abortive armed insurrection broke out in Moscow at the end of December, 1905. The immediate result of this policy was to produce a rift in the camp of the opposition. The liberals, organized now in the Constitutional Democratic party, were not willing to follow the lead of their unmanageable socialist allies; the two groups soon parted company. A division took place within the ranks of the liberals themselves and their moderate wing formed a separate party which took the name of the Octobrists. While the Cadets were anxious to fight for the extension of the newly-won political liberty, the Octobrists were completely satisfied with the October manifesto and did not want to go any further.

Generally speaking, a popular reaction against revolutionary excesses gradually set in, which in the end greatly helped the government. Many a landlord who but yesterday had applauded the resolutions of the Zemstvo conferences, now, after his estate had been burnt by the peasants, was ready to give up his liberalism and turn to the authorities for protection. Nor could one expect a factory owner whose income had been sadly reduced as a result of incessant labor disturbances to retain much of his original enthusiasm for the cause of political freedom. The population at large naturally was becoming tired of continuous excitement and was growing anxious to go back to a peaceful and settled existence. There was also a nationalistic reaction caused by the prominent part which had been played in the revolution by national minorities. One of its manifestations was the anti-Semitic movement, which assumed particularly large proportions in the western provinces of European Russia where the majority of the Jews were living. Anti-Jewish riots (the so-called "pogroms") took place in several regions; in some cases the police not only failed to suppress the disturbances, but actually sponsored and even provoked them.

In all this development the government found no little comfort. Its isolation had ended since, in addition to the opposition groups, there now existed conservative parties which were willing to support it, such as the Octobrists and the Nationalists, or the openly reactionary parties of the Right, favoring the restoration of the old order. With the active participation of local authorities there were formed in many cities the so-called Unions of the Russian People (or of the True Russians), which provided the illusion of a widespread popular support for autocracy. Most important of all, however, was the fact that the rank and file of the army proved to be still loyal to the monarchy. With the aid of troops the government engaged in an energetic suppression of disorders. Martial law was proclaimed in many provinces of the Empire, special "punitive expeditions" were sent out to particularly turbulent localities, and there were numerous arrests and executions. By 1907 order was restored throughout the country and the revolutionary organizations saw themselves reduced to impotence.

During the whole crisis the liberals remained in an extremely difficult position. Although they had been able to acquire a much wider social basis than they ever had possessed before, they still were not strong enough to con-

trol the situation. To achieve their end they had to co-
operate with other forces; yet they found it almost impossible to ally themselves permanently either with the
revolutionaries or with the government. Favoring the
road of peaceful evolution towards a democratic and parliamentary régime, the Cadets were out of sympathy with
the radical demands of the socialists as well as with their
revolutionary tactics. At the same time they distrusted
the government and suspected the sincerity of its constitutional pronouncements. To what extent their suspicions were justified is open to debate. It is true that
after its victory over the revolution the government re-
sisted the temptation to go back to the old order of things
and did not withdraw the constitution which had been
granted. But it is also true that it was losing no opportunity to make this constitution as harmless as possible,
and that many of its members, beginning with the Emperor himself, regretted the concession which had been
made under pressure.

It was in this atmosphere of mutual distrust and hostility that the State Duma, as the Russian representative
assembly was called, had to begin its activities. Elected
on the basis of a fairly democratic franchise, the first two
Dumas (1906 and 1907) had a brief and troublous
existence. Both were entirely controlled by the opposition and both were unwilling to coöperate with the government which, in its turn, found their demands far too
radical and utterly unacceptable. The inevitable result
in each case was the dissolution of the Duma after a very
short session. In June, 1907, the government finally decided to effect a drastic revision of the franchise by means
of an imperial decree. This amounted virtually to a
coup d'état as the Fundamental Laws, published in 1906,
stipulated the consent of the Duma for any change in the

electoral law. The procedure served its purpose, however, and the Third Duma, elected in 1907, had a safe
governmental majority. If the stormy career of the first
two Dumas can be viewed as an epilogue to the revolution
of 1905, with the Third Duma begins the history of the
Russian constitutional experiment.

THE DUMA AND THE GOVERNMENT

The political order established in Russia after the revolution of 1905 has often been described as "sham-consti-
tutionalism," and the Duma has been disparaged as a
mere "smoke-screen for autocracy" or a "convenient tool
in the hands of the government." For the prevalence of
this idea the representatives of the Russian opposition
must be held largely responsible. In the heat of their
struggle for a real parliamentary government it was natural for them to emphasize and even to exaggerate the
many limitations from which the work of the Duma had
to suffer. To a historian, however, the period appears in
a somewhat different light. Even if there was no parliament in Russia, there certainly was a constitutional
régime. And although the tsar retained his historical title
of autocrat, this was rather a mere verbal concession to
the centuries-old tradition and a glaring anachronism.
In reality his power was no longer absolute because it was
limited by the Fundamental Laws, which provided for
the obligatory concurrence of the Duma in legislation.
Strictly speaking, the Russian autocracy ceased to exist
with the publication of the manifesto of October 17,
1905.

Of course, it must be admitted that the Duma, as
finally established, was not a real parliament in the modern European sense of the word. To begin with, it did
not represent the whole people, being based on a limited

and unequal franchise which favored the large landowners and the city bourgeoisie to the detriment of the lower classes. National minorities also were discriminated against as compared with the purely Russian element of the population. Equally important were the limitations imposed upon the powers of the Duma. Under the Fundamental Laws, which could be changed only upon the initiative of the crown, the emperor enjoyed the exclusive right of directing foreign policy and the complete control of the executive. The ministers were responsible to him only and all the appointments both in the army and in the civil service were made in his name and required no further confirmation. Parts of the budget were declared to be "iron-clad," that is exempt from examination by the Duma. Article 87 of the Fundamental Laws reserved for the government the right to promulgate emergency legislation, in the intervals between the Duma sessions, by means of imperial decrees. This proved to be a convenient device to pass those measures which would meet with strong opposition. Although such laws had to be subsequently submitted to the Duma for ratification the latter, confronted in each case with an accomplished fact, usually found its freedom of action greatly hindered. Finally, to create one more check upon the activities of the Duma, the old bureaucratic Council of State was transformed into an upper chamber and its consent was made requisite for the passage of bills into laws. As only one half of its membership was elected, and that from public bodies representative of the upper groups of Russian society, while the other half was appointed by the crown, the Council of State could be counted upon to offer effective resistance should the Duma display an undesirable zeal for reform.

Yet one cannot discard the Duma as a negligible factor

in Russian political life after 1907. Of great importance
was the very fact that the principle of self-government
now was extended to the field of national administration,
from which heretofore it had been so consistently excluded. Moreover, in spite of all the above-mentioned
limitations, the Duma still was able to exercise a real influence upon the conduct of national affairs. Although, as
we have seen, it was not an adequate representation of
the Russian people, it nevertheless could voice the demands of independent public elements and from its trib-
une governmental policies could be subjected by the opposition to an outspoken criticism not subject to censorship and receiving the widest publicity possible. Nor was
the Duma entirely powerless in its relations with the
executive. It still retained the right to examine and vote
upon the greater part of the budget, and consequently
every minister who desired to pass his estimates through
the Duma was somewhat bound to seek its good will.
The other weapon in the hands of the legislative chamber
was its right of interpellation, that is, of asking explana-
tions from the heads of the executive departments. And
although, even in case of a unanimous censure, nothing
happened to the minister in question so long as he retained the confidence of his sovereign, the Russian
bureaucrats did not remain entirely insensitive to the attitude of popular representatives. As a matter of fact,
under the influence of the Duma many departments of
the central government became notably modernized and
liberalized.

Finally, during the few years of its peaceful existence
the Duma was able to pass various legislative measures
constituting in their entirety quite a creditable positive
achievement. A scheme of universal education was introduced and appropriations were voted for a corresponding

annual increase in the number of primary schools throughout the Empire. Measures were taken to endow the peasants with full civil rights, putting them on a basis of
equality with other classes; the office of "land captain"
was abolished and the jurisdiction of the justices of the
peace was extended to country districts. The Zemstvo
institutions were established in nine additional provinces,
important labor legislation was passed, and a very substantial improvement was achieved in the field of national
defense. To sum up, the Duma succeeded "in making itself an indispensable factor in the national life of Russia
and in retaining, in spite of all the obstacles in its way,
the vital essence inherent in the very principle of popular
representation" (Miliukov).

The relations between the Duma and the government
remained not very satisfactory even after the drastic
change in the electoral law which assured the preponderance of moderate elements in the legislative chamber.
The sponsor of this measure, Peter Stolypin, Prime Minister during 1906-11, hardly could be called a consistent
constitutionalist, in the strict sense of the word, as he sel-
dom hesitated to apply extra-constitutional methods
whenever he thought it necessary. It must be admitted,
however, that he sincerely valued the coöperation of the
Duma in legislative activity and had no thought of going
back to the old autocratic ways of governing Russia. A
man of upright character and great ability, he was hailed
by his admirers as "the Russian Bismarck" and denounced by the opposition as a high-handed reactionary.
To-day it is possible to appraise him calmly and without
exaggeration. That he was heart and soul in favor of
Russia's progress seems to be certain; to call him a reactionary would be obviously unjust. His agrarian policy[1]

---

[1] *Infra* pp. 81-83.

showed that he possessed both foresight and determination. But with all his outstanding qualities he lacked broad-mindedness and subtlety and thus fell short of becoming a really great statesman. In his methods he was often too dictatorial and he did not know how to manage men and parties. His end was tragic and in a way symbolical. In 1911 he was assassinated by an agent of the secret political police who at the same time was a member of a revolutionary organization. Only a few months before Stolypin had himself defended in the Duma the use as *agents-provocateurs* of such double-dealing persons, seeing in it a necessary weapon in the government's war on the revolutionaries.

After Stolypin's death the governmental policy towards the Duma became more inconsistent and vacillating. To the end of the imperial régime there was no unified cabinet in Russia, each minister being directly responsible to the emperor, with the Prime Minister occupying a position of merely honorary chairmanship. The result was that while some of the members of the government were more or less liberally inclined and desired to coöperate with the Duma, others were undisguised reactionaries and did not hesitate to display their hostility toward popular representation. With the emperor ill-suited to the rôle of constitutional monarch and not always willing to play the part at all, the reactionaries were able at times to get the upper hand in governmental councils and to place some irritating obstacles in the way of the legislative assembly. It was as a result of this policy that the moderate wing of the Duma gradually began to shift its position to the left until the way was prepared for a political understanding between the Cadets, on the one hand, and the Octobrists and even some of the Nationalists, on the other. The alignment of Duma parties on the eve of the

World War foreshadowed a new conflict between the constitutional opposition and the forces of reaction entrenched in the government. And of the two the opposition had a much better chance of success because it was supported by the general trend of Russia's social and intellectual evolution.

ECONOMIC ADVANCE DURING THE EARLY PART OF THE TWENTIETH CENTURY

In spite of the Russo-Japanese War and grave domestic troubles the early part of the twentieth century was for Russia a period of remarkable economic progress. After a brief interval caused by the revolution of 1905, when no regular productive activity was possible, Russian capitalism resumed its advance with renewed strength and increased rapidity. There was an extraordinary growth of production in the manufacture of textiles, in the metallurgical industry and in mining. Railroad building continued on a large scale until in 1912 Russia had a total mileage second only to that of the United States. Cities grew rapidly, and in 1914 the urban population formed 18 per cent of the whole population of the Empire, a substantial increase if compared with 13 per cent in 1897 and only 8 per cent in 1851. Although agriculture still remained the foundation of national economy, Russia was well on her way towards becoming an industrial country.

A characteristic feature of Russia's economic life in this period was the growth of industrial combinations, tending to control both production and marketing of goods in some of the principal branches of industry. This concentration of capital permitted the use of better technical methods and produced a striking improvement in the conditions which had prevailed during the earlier stages of the industrial development. Although the rôle played by the government in finance and industry continued to be a very important one, private initiative was asserting itself with more vigor than before; there was a notable tendency on the part of Russian industrialists to rely less on governmental subsidy and protection and more on their own resources. Simultaneously, a significant change was taking place in the relationship between the foreign and domestic capital invested in Russian industry. If at the beginning of the twentieth century the predominance in the field still belonged to foreign capital, by 1910 conditions had become radically different and native capital was gaining a clear ascendancy. There could no longer be any doubt that capitalism had taken firm roots in the economic life of the country and that it had proven its vitality.

No less important was the development in the field of agriculture. Here, too, there was a steady increase in production, although not so spectacular as in some branches of industry. A significant phenomenon was the success of capitalistic agriculture, which could organize large-scale production and obtain, by using technical improvements, a much higher yield from its farming than was possible for the average peasant. The latter was still hindered by his open field system, his backward methods of cultivation and his lack of capital. Large-scale farming, concentrating on the production of the more valuable crops, was responsible for a very considerable part of Russia's agricultural export.

So long, however, as the bulk of the peasantry remained little affected by the general economic progress, the agrarian problem could not be considered as solved and the whole national economy lacked a permanent and a stable foundation. The outstanding importance of the problem was equally appreciated by the government and by the opposition, but the methods by which they wanted to approach its solution were widely different. The most radical proposal emanated from the Social Revolutionaries who insisted on nationalization of land as the panacea for Russia's economic evils. A more moderate program was formulated by the Constitutional Democrats: it contemplated the distribution among the peasants of all the land belonging to the state, the crown and the monasteries, and the compulsory alienation of some part of the privately owned land, again for the benefit of the peasants; for the loss of their property the landlords were to be compensated by the government at an "equitable price."

To this and similar proposals the government answered with categorical objections. Its spokesmen insisted, and not without reason, that even if all the land available for agriculture were divided among the peasants the actual increase in their holdings would be comparatively insignificant and thus would fail to bring about a substantial improvement. The government refused also to violate the principle of private property. It expressed great concern for the fate of large-scale farming in Russia, indispensable as it was for the general economic progress of the country. Under the leadership of Stolypin it advanced an agrarian program of its own, designed to improve the conditions of the peasantry without attacking private property or compromising the success of capitalistic agriculture. The governmental program did not exclude, however, the extension of peasant landownership. In 1905 the State Land Bank for the Peasants, whose operations up to that time had been conducted on a rather limited scale, was given greatly increased powers which permitted it to become a very effective instrument of an active agrarian policy. Considerable tracts of state and crown land were sold through the Bank to the peasants.

Numerous estates of private landowners, many of whom were greatly frightened by the agrarian riots of 1905, likewise passed into the hands of the peasants with the financial assistance of the Bank. The area of land which the Bank had helped the peasants to buy during the period 1883-1912 reached an aggregate of about 43 million acres, a record that can hardly be paralleled in the history of any other country.

Another important item in the governmental program was organized assistance to peasant migration from the congested rural districts of European Russia into the thinly populated Asiatic provinces of the Empire. Here again it was not until 1905 that the policy of assistance assumed really large proportions, commensurate with the importance of the task. Special scientific expeditions were periodically sent out by the Colonization Department of the Ministry of Agriculture to various parts of Asiatic Russia for a survey of suitable areas and every year the agents of the Department prepared for settlement extensive tracts of land mostly in Siberia. The settlers were granted land in perpetual use against the payment of a small rent and they were entitled also to a number of other privileges such as reduced railroad fares, loans for traveling expenses, and temporary remission of taxes. Moreover, both in European Russia and in the regions of new settlement the government developed a fairly efficient system of expert agricultural assistance in coöperation with the Zemstvos, which likewise paid great attention to this problem. By 1914 there were about ten thousand agricultural experts in Russia, regularly engaged in helping the peasant to improve his methods of cultivation.

The very core of Stolypin's agrarian program, however, was the legislation dealing with the village commune

(1906-1911). A direct reversal of the previous governmental policy, it aimed at a gradual elimination of the commune and the encouragement of individual landownership among the Russian peasants. Under the terms of the Stolypin laws every member of the commune had the right to claim his share in the common land of the village as his private property. The next step was the actual enclosure of the land thus appropriated; this would permit the owner to have his land in one compact holding and not in widely scattered strips as under the open field system. Stolypin's aim in promoting this legislation was both of an economic and political nature: he objected to the commune as an obstacle in the way of agricultural progress and he wanted to create in Russia a numerous class of small landed proprietors, constituting both a conservative force and a bulwark against revolution.

In the heat of their struggle against the government the members of the opposition vigorously attacked the laws of 1906-1911 as a mere political stratagem on the part of Stolypin and as an example of high-handed bureaucratic interference with popular customs. They insisted also that this policy favored the wealthy peasants to the detriment of the others. Viewed in historical perspective, however, the agrarian legislation of Stolypin appears as a decidedly progressive measure. It was in complete harmony with the general capitalistic development of the country. For some time social differentiation had been going on in the villages, individualist tendencies had been coming to the fore, and the commune had been rapidly losing its vitality. It was because of this general background that the Stolypin legislation achieved rather striking results during the short period of time when it was in operation. By the end of 1913 about 24 per cent of all the peasant households in European Russia had availed themselves of the opportunity to appropriate their communal holdings on the basis of individual ownership.

On the eve of the World War the agrarian problem in Russia was still far from being solved, but it was at least on its way to solution. The peasants had in their hands over 75 per cent of all the arable land in the country; personal initiative was liberated from the deadening influence of the commune; the financial burden of the peasantry had been greatly alleviated by the cancellation in 1906 of the balance of the redemption payments; agricultural improvements were being made available to the small farmer by the activities of the Zemstvos and the government; a greater opportunity existed for increased earnings in connection with the general progress of national economy. Still another beneficial factor of prime importance was the prodigious growth in Russia of the coöperative movement. In 1914 there were in the country over thirty thousand coöperative societies of various descriptions with a predominantly rural membership. The movement helped the peasants to adapt themselves to new economic conditions, taught them self-reliance and group solidarity, and gave them direct material advantages by substantially reducing the part of the middleman. Although complete and reliable statistical data are not available and allowance must be made for great variety in local conditions, there can be no doubt that on the whole the Russian countryside was growing more prosperous and the peasants' standard of living was gradually rising.

Labor conditions in the urban centers likewise represented a substantial improvement upon the state of affairs which had prevailed during the preceding period. In 1912 the Duma passed legislation which established health and accident insurance for the workers. Wages were steadily rising, particularly in St. Petersburg and in Moscow, while in many factories where they remained rather low the policy was established of supplementing wages with free lodgings, medical services and educational facilities. In 1906 the organization of labor unions on a large scale had finally been permitted by law and, although the government had immediately started to restrict their development, some of them managed to survive and were able to exercise a certain influence upon the employers. Among the latter there was growing a type of "enlightened industrialist," who was much more concerned in the welfare of his workers than the early pioneers of Russian capitalism had ever thought of being. Neither in the cities nor in the villages was this improvement in the conditions of the working masses radical enough to dispel at once the popular discontent which had been accumulating for centuries, but it was at least an indication that the country's social problems could find eventually a peaceful solution.

CULTURAL PROGRESS UNDER THE CONSTITUTIONAL RÉGIME

Not only the body but the soul of Russia as well was growing stronger and healthier during the decade which preceded the World War. Progress in the field of education was no less striking than that on the economic side. The most pressing problem was to reduce in the shortest time possible the appallingly high percentage of illiteracy which still prevailed within the country. The Duma, the government and the Zemstvos applied themselves to the task with an energy and a determination that were without precedent in Russian history. It was only in this period that elementary education in Russia was finally put on a firm basis. In 1908, when the scheme of universal education was first advanced as a practical proposition, there had been somewhat less than one hundred thousand primary schools in the country. By the end of 1913 this figure was increased to one hundred and fifty thousand and definite plans were worked out to establish during the following decade a number of new schools sufficient to take care of every child in the Empire. The realization of this plan was made more or less secure by correspondingly large appropriations: in 1914 the expenses for popular education showed an increase of 628 per cent over the budget of 1894.

In the secondary schools and the universities (of which there were now eleven as compared with six in the first half of the nineteenth century) the number of students had increased rapidly; at the same time these educational institutions were becoming more and more accessible to the lower classes. There was also notable progress as far as freedom of teaching was concerned. Even in the secondary schools political pressure on the part of the government became hardly noticeable. The universities which, since the publication of the new statute of 1905, had been governed by their own faculties on the basis of academic autonomy, enjoyed a practically complete freedom of teaching. There were still occasional sharp conflicts between the universities and the government, but these conflicts arose almost invariably out of the political activities of the students and had nothing to do with the character of instruction.

Generally speaking, the constitutional régime brought with it a very considerable relaxation of governmental censorship. To be sure, during the period of reaction which followed the revolution of 1905 the censor still remained very active, but if compared with the preceding period his efforts were neither so far-reaching nor so effective. The revolutionary events stimulated discussion of political and social subjects and this continued even after the suppression of the revolution. The daily press occupied now a much more important place in national life than ever before and the opposition newspapers were able, in spite of all the obstacles in their way, to present their views and to influence public opinion. A similar phenomenon of great importance was the progress of religious toleration. A law published in 1905 made religious affiliation a matter of free choice with every Russian citizen and gave the "old believers" and the sectarians a legal status, although still retaining the privileged position of the Greek Orthodox Church. In the ranks of the latter voices began to be heard in favor of liberating the church from governmental control; a significant movement started among the laity and the clergy aiming at the convocation of a church council and the reëstablishment of the Patriarchate.

One of the beneficial results of the constitutional reform was the emancipation of the intellectual life of educated Russia from the exclusive domination of politics. With the establishment of the Duma, the formation of legally recognized parties and the relaxation of censorship, a wider outlet was created for political energy and interest. This permitted the other fields of intellectual activity to regain their independence. Pure science, art for art's sake, and abstract philosophical thinking were reëstablished in a position of honor and ceased to be looked upon as mere reactionary devices, designed to divert public opinion from consideration of civic problems. The somewhat narrow and intolerant creed of the radical *intelligentsia* began to lose its unity and vitality. Intellectual life became more diversified; new and highly interesting tendencies were manifesting themselves both in literature and in art. A poetical renaissance took place with the appearance in Russia of the symbolist school, which exercised also a considerable influence on the Russian novel and drama. Literary criticism was divorced from political and social propaganda; a complete revision of literary values was undertaken from a purely artistic point of view. There was a similar development in Russian painting, which became more concerned with the quest for beauty and less willing to serve any purpose other than its own.

Among those who still remained true to the ideal of civic duty there were also noticeable some significant changes. It looked as if the professional revolutionary, with his peculiar psychology shaped by underground activities, was rapidly becoming a thing of the past. In place of a self-appointed savior of humanity, a type to which so many of the old intellectuals belonged, there was now appearing the expert, ready to apply his special knowledge wherever it was needed. The whole relationship between the *intelligentsia* and the popular masses was gradually assuming a more normal character. On the part of the intellectuals there was less of a somewhat morbid desire to atone for the sins of their fathers by a self-denying ministry to the "people," while the masses themselves were just beginning to lose their deep-seated distrust of the educated man as a member of the privileged minority. The formation of a new layer of the *intelligentsia,* actually coming from the lower classes, promised to play a most important part in this connection. This development was only in its early stages; there still remained a dangerously wide gulf separating the educated class of Russia from the majority of the nation.

THE WORLD WAR AND THE FALL OF THE IMPERIAL GOVERNMENT

The war came for Russia at the most inopportune time, when she needed every ounce of her energy for the work of internal reorganization. It interrupted that political, economic, and cultural progress which has been described in the preceding sections; it imposed upon the Empire an overwhelming burden before the latter had an opportunity to establish itself firmly on new and stronger foundations.

Much has been written about the military unpreparedness of Russia at the time of her entrance into the war. One should be careful, however, not to exaggerate the importance of this factor. There had been a very substantial improvement in the organization and equipment of the Russian army since the Japanese War, and in 1914, whatever were its deficiencies, this army was a formidable fighting machine. Russia's unpreparedness was much more economic than military. After all, from the purely military point of view, not a single country participating in the war, not even Germany, was adequately prepared for a conflict of such magnitude and duration. But while Germany, England, and France, because of their more developed economic system, were able to adjust themselves to the exigencies of the war in a comparatively short period of time, it took Russia much longer to perform this feat and the sacrifices she had to make were correspondingly larger than those of any other country. It was only in the beginning of 1917 that the Russian army became adequately supplied with ammunition necessary to enable it to undertake large-scale offensive operations with a reasonable assurance of lasting success. But by that time the best human material had been spent in previous efforts, Russia's losses had reached an appallingly high total, the morale of the nation had been undermined by several years of intense suffering, and the country was on the eve of a revolution. To the difficulties at the front was added the disorganization in the rear. The blockade, the repeated mobilizations of the able-bodied male population of the country (over 15 million men were mobilized in Russia during the war), and the breakdown of the railroad system under the heavy burden imposed on it by the transportation of troops and supplies, combined to produce an acute economic crisis. Factories could not secure enough fuel and there was a shortage of food in the urban centers of the Empire.

Most ominous of all, however, was the political crisis which made any concerted national effort actually impossible. In the beginning of the war the Russian government for a while had behind it a united nation. The war was undoubtedly popular with the educated classes and the urban population at large. It was conceived to be one of national defense against an unprovoked aggression. There was enough of sympathy for the cause of the Balkan Slavs, Russia's kin by race and religion, to support the idea that Serbia could not be abandoned to her fate. For the liberals, coöperation with France and England was extremely welcome, while they saw in the "Prussianized" Germany a bulwark of militarism and reaction. Immediately upon the declaration of war the representatives of the opposition in the Duma solemnly promised the government their full support and expressed their readiness to postpone all domestic quarrels. The masses of the people in the country districts, while not displaying any enthusiasm, accepted the war as inevitable and were prepared to do their duty.

To the general offer of reconciliation and coöperation made by the various elements of the Russian people the government failed to give any adequate response. In one of the most trying moments of Russian history it behaved as if nothing had happened. No changes were made either in the personnel of the government or in administrative practices. The reactionary ministers were still obviously hostile toward the Duma and all independent public bodies. Under such conditions the honeymoon of patriotic coöperation could not last very long. In the summer of 1915, under the influence of a staggering military defeat, the political discontent which had been accumulating during the first year of the war again became loud and outspoken. For the time being the government saw itself forced to make concessions. Some of the most unpopular ministers were replaced by persons more acceptable to the Duma. Simultaneously, the legislative chambers and public organizations such as the Zemstvos, the municipalities, and the newly-formed War Industry Committees, were admitted to direct participation in the work of supplying the army with ammunition. Subsequent events showed, however, that this was not a radical change of policy on the part of the government. The emperor's decision to take over the high command of the army and his departure for the front marked the beginning of the ascendancy of the empress in the direction of national affairs. A firm believer in autocracy, Empress Alexandra was possessed by an almost unlimited hatred for the Duma and the opposition, while her morbid mysticism made her an easy prey for the notorious Rasputin, whose influence upon her became supreme. Under a strong pressure on the part of the empress and her advisor, Nicholas II blindly started upon the road of his own destruction. The Duma was consistently slighted and neglected; other public bodies continued to be looked upon with profound suspicion. One by one the more liberal ministers were forced out of the government, being replaced by reactionaries, many of whom were generally known to be Rasputin's nominees. Unusually frequent changes, all based on the passing whims of those in power, took place in the personnel of the cabinet; governmental policy soon lost even the semblance of any unity or vigor.

The Duma tried to save the situation by repeated appeals to the sovereign in favor of a more reasonable policy for the sake of national defense. A coalition of all parties, except the extreme reactionaries and the radical socialists, was formed under the name of the Progressive Bloc and advanced a moderate and statesmanlike program: it demanded a unified cabinet composed of men enjoying the confidence of the country and a more liberal policy which would eliminate the conflict between the government and public opinion. Unless this program was accepted, the Duma saw no possibility for Russia to win the war. Other warnings came from the Zemstvo and municipal organizations, from the Council of State and from the Union of the Nobility, finally even from some members of the imperial family. To all these admonitions the emperor remained entirely deaf.

In the fall of 1916 the situation became well-nigh unbearable. The government was completely isolated and universally distrusted. Ugly rumors began to circulate all over Russia. It was believed, without sufficient foundation as we now know, that the empress, Rasputin, and their nominees were preparing to deliver the country into the hands of the Germans. These rumors reached the army and undermined the morale of the soldiers. Gloom and depression reigned everywhere. The general feeling was that the country had reached an *impasse* from which

some way out had to be found. In December of 1916 a
small group of aristocratic conspirators assassinated Rasputin, but this act failed to improve the situation. Plans
of a palace *coup d'état* were under way, but before they
could materialize a popular revolution, vaguely antici-
pated by everybody and prepared by no one, broke out
in St. Petersburg. It began late in February, 1917, with
isolated food riots in various parts of the city, followed
by a general revolt of the reserve battalions stationed in
the capital. It probably would have remained an un-
organized local outbreak had it not been given the stamp
of approval by the Duma. In the face of complete chaos
in the capital the Duma reluctantly decided to take over
the reins of government from the hands of the tsarist
ministers who abandoned them without any struggle.
The change was immediately accepted both by the army
and the whole population of the Empire. Pending the
convocation of a Constituent Assembly, a Provisional
Government was formed on the basis of an agreement between the Duma and the Soviet of Workmen's and Soldiers' Deputies hastily organized by the socialist parties.
Abandoned by everybody, Nicholas II abdicated for himself and the heir to the throne in favor of his brother,
Grand Duke Michael, who in turn declined to accept
power until the decision of the Constituent Assembly
should be reached. This meant the end of the Russian
monarchy. It took only a few days to overthrow a dynasty which had existed for more than three centuries. In
the words of a Russian political leader, the monarchy had
actually committed suicide.

CONCLUSION

Imperial Russia is now a thing of the past. An historian should attempt to view it in its entirety and to

approach it with necessary detachment. Its record is not one of unmitigated evil; it has to its credit many outstanding positive achievements. Moreover, at the time of its fall it was by no means beyond the hope of regeneration. During the period which forms the subject of this study the Russian imperial régime did not remain unchanged but on the contrary was undergoing a process of constant modification. Reforms usually came too late and, as a rule, were followed by periods of reaction, but on the whole it was a forward movement, not a retrogression. On the eve of the World War Russia was profoundly different from what she had been in the beginning of the nineteenth century. In spite of the deadweight of the past and the acute contradictions of the present, it was a steadily and rapidly progressing country. In view of this progress it would be hardly correct to assert that the revolution was absolutely inevitable. Russia still had to solve many complicated and difficult problems but the possibility of their peaceful solution was by no means excluded. To the extent that the country was growing economically more prosperous and culturally more advanced, this possibility was constantly gaining strength and the danger of a violent upheaval was becoming more remote.

To this hope of peaceful evolution the war dealt a staggering blow. It caught Russia in the very process of radical internal reorganization. The constitutional experiment was less than a decade old; the agrarian legislation of Stolypin had been in operation for a few years only; the scheme of universal education was just beginning to be realized; the industrial development, rapid as it was, had not yet passed beyond its early stages. Under such conditions the war was bound to produce grave disturbances in the internal life of the country. A heroic and concerted effort on the part of the whole nation was needed if the imperial structure was to weather the storm. To such an indispensable effort, the political crisis of 1915-1917 was an insurmountable obstacle.   The war made the revolution highly probable, but human folly made it inevitable.

AUTHOR'S NOTE

THE aim of this study has been to give an account of the fundamental factors in Russian historical evolution from the beginning of the nineteenth century to the revolution of 1917. Foreign policy, for lack of space, has been included in the discussion only in those cases in which it affected directly the internal development of the country.

All dates are given in accordance with the old Russian calendar which remained in force until 1918.

The author is grateful for the friendly assistance of his colleagues, Professor Rupert Emerson and Mr. M. T. B. Spalding, in the revision of his manuscript.

BIBLIOGRAPHICAL NOTE

This bibliographical note contains only a selected list of works available in English; more complete lists of titles may be found in George M. Dutcher *et al., Guide to Historical Literature* (2d ed.; New York, 1961); Robert J. Kerner, *Slavic Europe: A Selected Bibliography in the West European Languages, Compromising History, Languages and Literature* (Cambridge, Mass., 1918); Charles Morley, *Guide to Research in Russian History* (Syracuse, N.Y., 1951); and Pushkarev's work listed below.

Among the many outstanding textbooks on Russian history, the following are recommended for their material on Russia, 1801–1917: Michael Florinsky, *Russia: A History and an Interpretation*, 2 vols. (New York, 1953, 1955), the second volume covers the nineteenth and twentieth centuries; Benedict H. Sumner, *A Short History of Russia* (rev. ed.; New York, 1949), topically arranged; Melvin Wren, *The Course of Russian History* (3d ed.; New York, 1968); Sir Bernard Pares, *A History of Russia* (def. ed.; New York, 1960), a classic history; Hugh Seton-Watson, *The Russian Empire 1801–1917* (London and New York, 1967), thorough and objective; Sergei Pushkarev, *The Emergence of Modern Russia, 1801–1917* (New York, 1963), very helpful bibliography; George Vernadsky, *A History of Russia* (5th rev. ed.; New Haven, Conn., 1961); and A. Kornilov, *Modern Russian History from the Age of Catherine the Great to the End of the Nineteenth Century* (New York, 1952). For a documentary collection, there is Warren B. Walsh (ed.),

Readings in Russian History, paperback, 3 vols. (Syracuse, N.Y., 1963). As a reference on all aspects of Russian history, consult Michael T. Florinsky (ed.), *McGraw-Hill Encyclopedia of Russia and the Soviet Union* (New York, 1961). An excellent survey of Russian economic history can be found in the chapters by Michael Karpovich in Witt Bowden, Michael Karpovich, and Abbott Payson Usher, *An Economic History of Europe since 1750* (New York, 1937). There is valuable information on Russian economic history in the older James Mavor, *An Economic History of Russia,* 2 vols. (New York, 1925). For Russian thought in the nineteenth century, see Thomas G. Masaryk, *The Spirit of Russia,* 3 vols. (New York, 1955, 1968), and V. V. Zenkovsky, *A History of Russian Philosophy,* 2 vols. (New York, 1953). On Russian literature, there is D. S. Mirsky, *History of Russian Literature: From its Beginnings to 1900,* paperback (New York, 1960). Works on Russian music include Richard A. Leonard, *A History of Russian Music* (New York, 1957); Montagu Montagu-Nathan, *A History of Russian Music* (London, 1918); and Rosa Newmarch, *The Russian Opera* (London, 1914).

For political thought, read Hans Kohn (ed.), *The Mind of Modern Russia. Historical and Political Thought of Russsia's Great Age (1825–1917),* paperback (New York, 1961). A valuable work on the Russian peasantry is Jerome Blum, *Lord and Peasant in Russia from the Ninth to the Nineteenth Century* (Princeton, N.J., 1961). For the history of rural Russia, see Geroid T. Robinson, *Rural Russia under the Old Regime,* paperback (Berkeley, Calif., 1967). Populism and the revolutionary movement are dealt with in Franco Venturei, *Roots of Revolution: A History of the Populist and Socialist Movements in Nineteenth Century Russia* (New York, 1960); and Avraham

Yarmolinsky, *Road to Revolution: A Century of Russian Radicalism* (New York, 1959).

Biographies of the tsars include Leonid I. Strakhovsky, *Alexander I of Russia: the Man Who Defeated Napoleon* (New York, 1947); E. M. Almedingen, *The Emperor Alexander I* (New York, 1963); Constantine de Grunwald, *Tsar Nicholas I* (New York, 1954); and Marc Raeff, *Michael Speransky, Statesmen of Imperial Russia, 1771–1839* (The Hague, 1957). Anatole G. Mazour, *The First Russian Revolution, 1825: the Decembrist Movement* (Stanford, Calif., 1961) and Mikail, Zetlin, *The Decembrists* (New York, 1958) are both useful.

Important aspects of the reign of Nicholas I are analyzed in Walter McKenzie Pintner, *Russian Economic Policy under Nicholas I* (Ithaca, N.Y., 1967); John Shelton Curtiss, *The Russian Army under Nicholas I, 1825–1855* (Durham, N.C., 1965); Nicholas V. Riasanovsky, *Nicholas I and Official Nationality in Russia, 1825–1855* (Berkeley, Calif., 1959); and Sidney Monas, *The Third Section: Police and Society in Russia under Nicholas I* (Cambridge, Mass., 1961), an absorbing work.

Broader studies can be found in John S. Curtiss (ed.), *The Peasant in Nineteenth Century Russia* (Stanford, Calif., 1968); William L. Blackwell, *The Beginnings of Russian Industrialization, 1800–1860* (Princeton, N.J., 1968); Nicholas Riasanovsky, *Russia and the West in the Teaching of the Slavophiles: A Study of Romantic Ideology* (Cambridge, Mass., 1952); and Stuart R. Tompkins, *The Russian Mind: From Peter the Great Through the Enlightenment* (Norman, Okla., 1957).

Alexander Herzen, *My Past and Thoughts,* 6 vols. (London, 1924–1927), is not only a literary masterpiece but also an important historical document. For Herzen's career and his influence on socialism, see Martin E. Malia, *Alexander Herzen and the Birth of Russian Socialism, 1812–1885* (Cambridge, Mass., 1961).

CHAPTER II

Hugh Seton-Watson, *The Decline of Imperial Russia, 1855–1914,* paperback (New York, 1961), is a first-rate survey.

Biographies include E. M. Almendingen, *The Emperor Alexander II* (London, 1962); Stephen Graham, *Tsar of Freedom: The Life and Reign of Alexander II* (New Haven, Conn., 1935); Werner E. Mosse, *Alexander II and the Modernization of Russia* (New York, 1958), excellent, short account; Robert F. Byrnes, *Pobedonostsev: His Life and Thought* (Bloomington, Ind., 1968), a penetrating study; and Richard Hare, *Portraits of Russian Personalities Between Reform and Revolution* (New York, 1959), sketches of Pobedonostsev, Witte, and Stolypin.

For political institutions consult Jacob Walkin, *The Rise of Democracy in Pre-Revolutionary Russia: Political and Social Institutions under the Last Three Czars* (New York, 1962). The legal system is treated in a thorough study, Samuel Kucherov, *Courts, Lawyers, and Trials under the Last Three Czars* (New York, 1953). Theodore H. von Laue, *Sergei Witte and the Industrialization of Russia* (New York, 1963) is useful. There have been excellent studies of aspects of the revolutionary movement, including David Footman, *Red Prelude: the Life of the Russian Terrorist Zhelyabov* (New Haven, Conn., 1945), dealing with the assassination of Alexander II; Richard Wortman, *The Crisis of Russian Populism* (New York, 1967).

Accounts of Marxism and Russian Marxists are Samuel H. Baron, *Plekhanov: the Father of Russian Marxism* (Stanford, Calif., 1963); Leopold H. Haimson, *The Russian Marxists and the Origins of Bolshevism* (Cambridge, Mass., 1955); Donald W. Treadgold, *Lenin and His Rivals* (New York, 1955); Richard Pipes, *Social Democracy and the St. Petersburg Labor Movement, 1885–1897* (Cambridge, Mass., 1963); Arthur P. Mendel, *Dilemmas of Progress in Tsarist Russia: Legal Marxism and Legal Populism* (Cambridge, Mass. 1961); Richard Kindersley, *The First Russian Revisionists: a Study of "Legal Marxism" in Russia* (New York, 1962); and the classic Bertram D. Wolfe, *Three Who Made a Revolution* (New York, 1948), the early careers of Lenin, Trotsky, and Stalin.

Pan-Slavism is treated in Michael B. Petrovich, *The Emergence of Russian Panslavism, 1856–1870* (New York, 1965) and Hans Kohn, *Panslavism: Its History and Ideology* (2d edition; New York, 1960). Stuart R. Tompkins, *The Russian Intelligentsia: Makers of the Revolutionary State* (Norman, Okla., 1957) is important for the years 1855–1917. For agricultural history, see G. Pavsolsky, *Agricultural Russia on the Eve of the Revolution* (New York, 1949). For Russian social history, there is Cyril Black (ed.), *The Transformation of Russian Society: Aspects of Social Change since 1861* (Cambridge, Mass., 1960).

D. M. Wallace, *Russia on the Eve of War and Revolution* (rev. ed.; New York, 1961) is a classic description of postreform Russia. Sir John Maynard's works, *Russia in Flux: Before October,* paperback (New York, 1946) and *The Russian Peasant and Other Studies,* paperback (New York, 1948) are useful for their insight into the history of the Russian people.

Among the accounts about the reign of the last of the tsars there are Richard Charques, *The Twilight of Imperial Russia* (London, 1958); Robert K. Massie, *Nicholas and Alexandra* (New York, 1967), with emphasis on family life; and Henri Troyat, *Daily Life in Russia Under the Last Tsar* (New York, 1962).

The history of the church is detailed in John S. Curtiss, *Church and State in Russia: the Last Years of the Empire, 1900–1917* (New York, 1940). On the Duma, consult Alfred Levin, *The Second Duma: A Study of the Social-Democratic Party and the Russian Constitutional Experiment* (New Haven, Conn., 1940) and Serge Levitsky, *The Russian Duma: Studies in Parliamentary Procedure, 1906–1917* (New York, 1958). Sidney Harcave, *First Blood: the Russian Revolution of 1905* (New York, 1964) is a valuable study based on thorough research. Sir Bernard Pares, *The Fall of the Russian Monarchy: A Study of the Evidence,* paperback (New York, 1961) and Michael T. Florinsky, *The End of the Russian Empire,* paperback (New York, 1961) are classic works on the collapse of the tsarist government. A significant study on the role of the anarchists is Paul Avrich, *The Russian Anarchists* (Princeton, N.J., 1967). Frank Alfred Golder (ed.), *Documents of Russian History 1914–1917* (New York, 1927) is a useful collection of original materials. Richard Hough, *The Potemkin Mutiny* (New York, 1962) is a good naval yarn that is well written.

From among the many memoirs of the last tsar's reign the following are helpful: Sir George Buchanan, *My Mission to Russia and Other Diplomatic Memoirs,* 2 vols. (Boston, 1923); George T. Marye, *Nearing the End in Imperial Russia* (Philadelphia, 1919), the memoirs of the

American ambassador; Maurice Paleologue, *An Ambassador's Memoirs,* 3 vols. (New York, 1923–1925); M. V. Rodzianko, *The Reign of Rasputin: An Empire's Collapse* (New York, 1927), the memoirs of the last Duma president; V. N. Kokovtsov, *Out of My Past: the Memoirs of Count Kokovtsov, Russian Minister of Finance, 1904–1914, chairman of the Council of Ministers, 1911–1914* (Stanford, Calif., 1934); and Sir Bernard Pares, *My Russian Memoirs, 1898–1919* (London, 1931), important.

The Carnegie Endowment for International Peace published the Russian Series of the Economic and Social History of the World War, and among the outstanding volumes in this series are (including the Florinsky, *The End of the Russian Empire* which is the concluding volume), N. I. Artrov and P. P. Gronsky, *The War and the Russian Government* (New Haven, Conn., 1919); T. I. Polner, *Russian Local Government during the War and the Union of Zemstvos* (New Haven, Conn., 1930); N. N. Golovine, *The Russian Army in the World War* (New Haven, Conn., 1931); B. E. Nolde, *Russia in the Economic War* (New Haven. Conn., 1928); and Alexis N. Antsiferov, Alexander D. Bilimovich *et al, Russian Agriculture During the War* (New Haven, Conn., 1930).

INDEX

105

INDEX